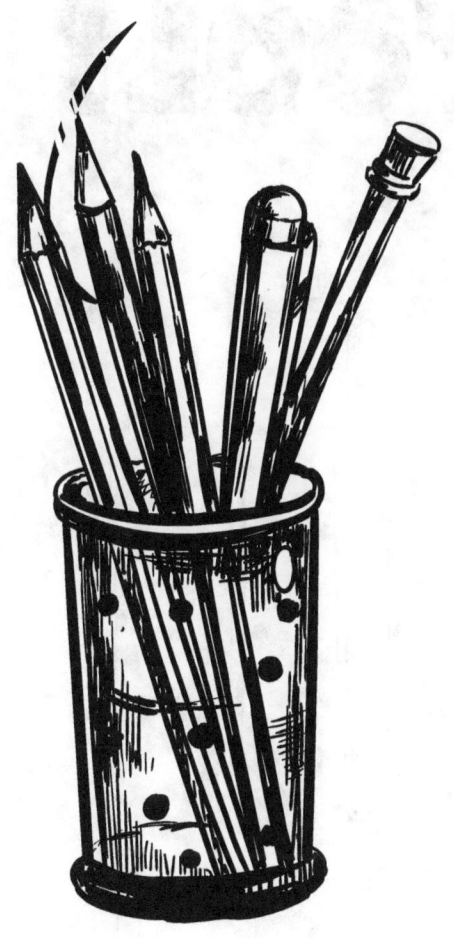

Drawing has rules, the most important of which is to look carefully at the shape that you want to draw, before you start drawing.
You can use several tools like:
Pencils, pens, colored pens, etc...
Then simplify drawing with geometric shapes, as in this book
And if you want to learn, you have to draw every day.

TOOLS

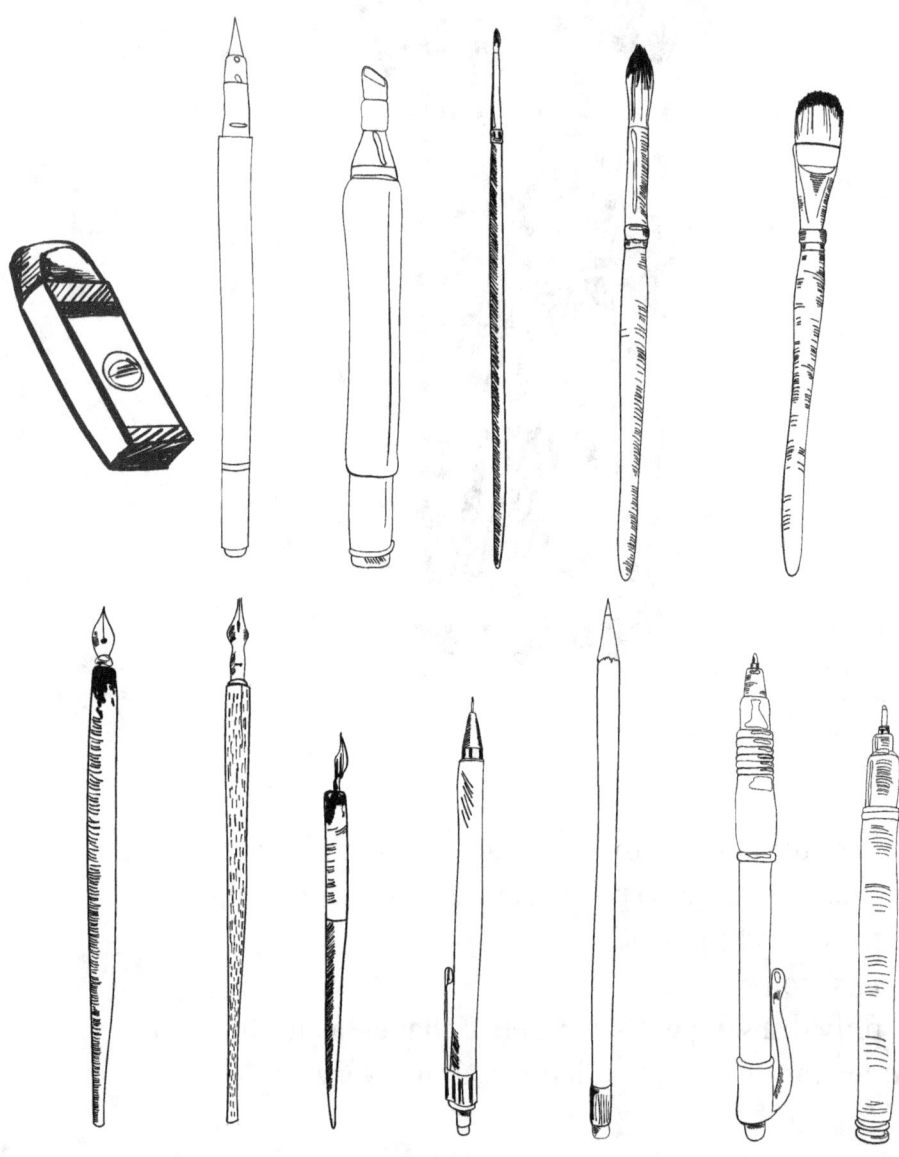

HOW TO DRAW

DRAWING TUTORIAL FOLWERS

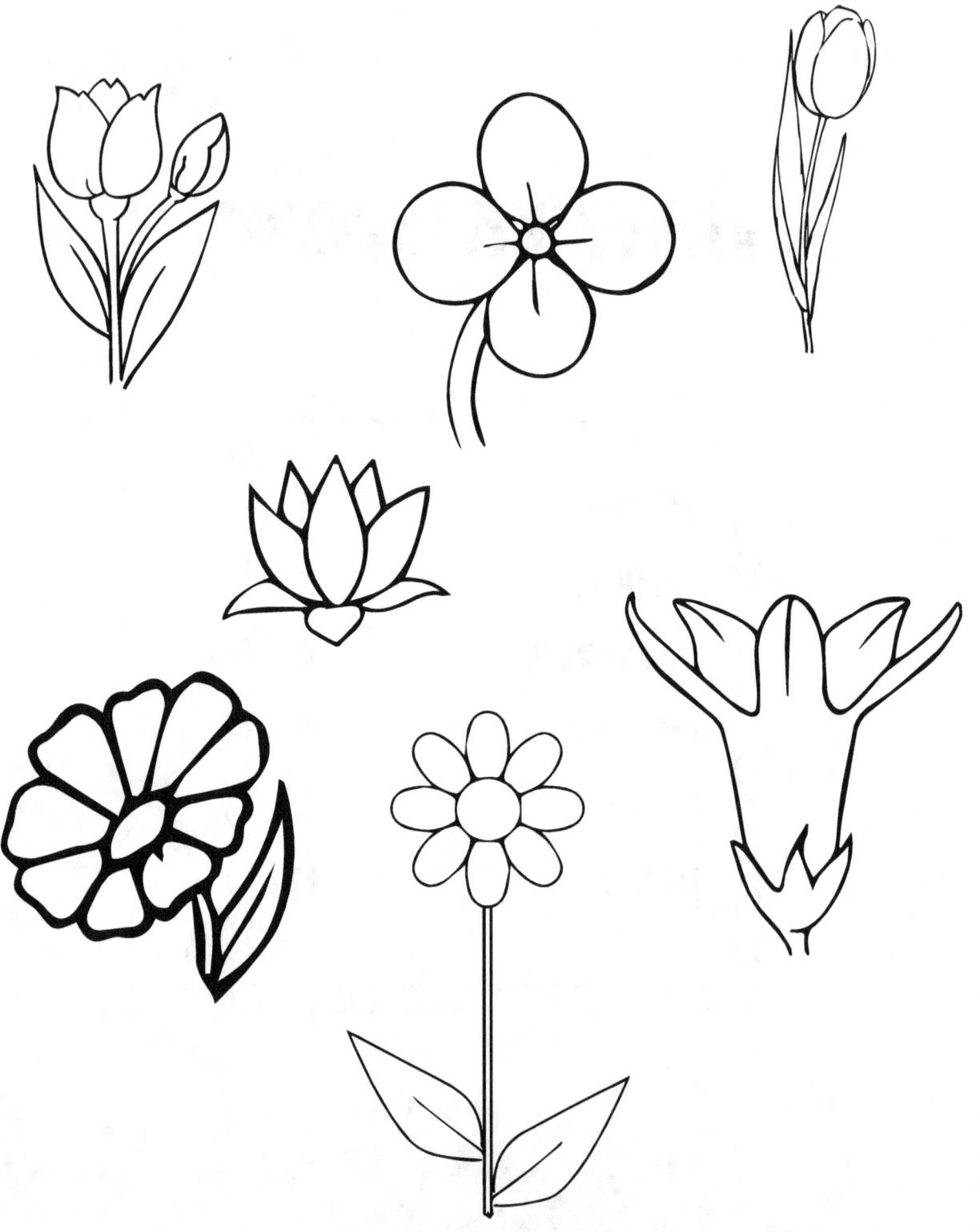

Look at the steps	Draw over the drawing	Repeat the drawing here

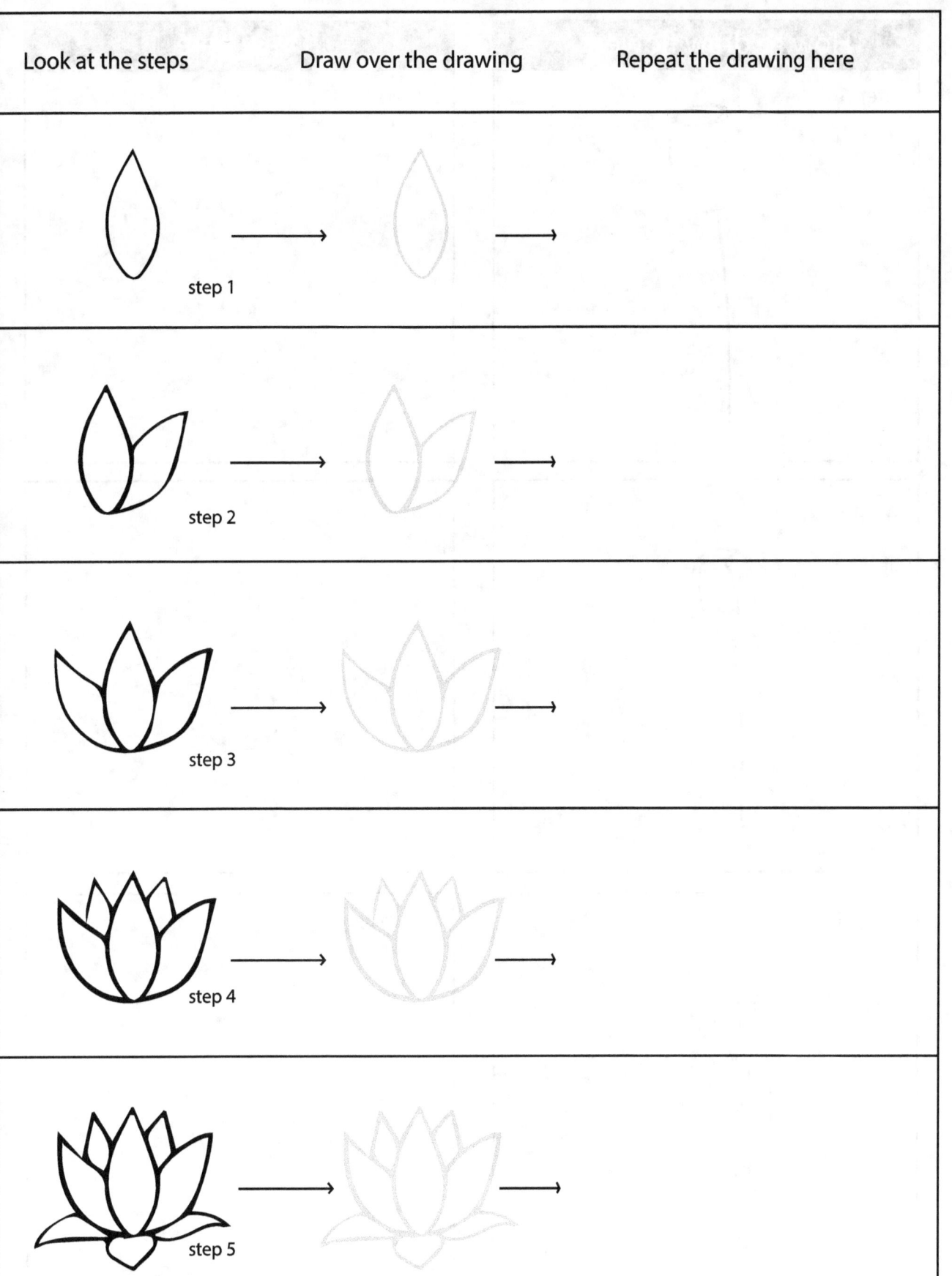

step 1

step 2

step 3

step 4

step 5

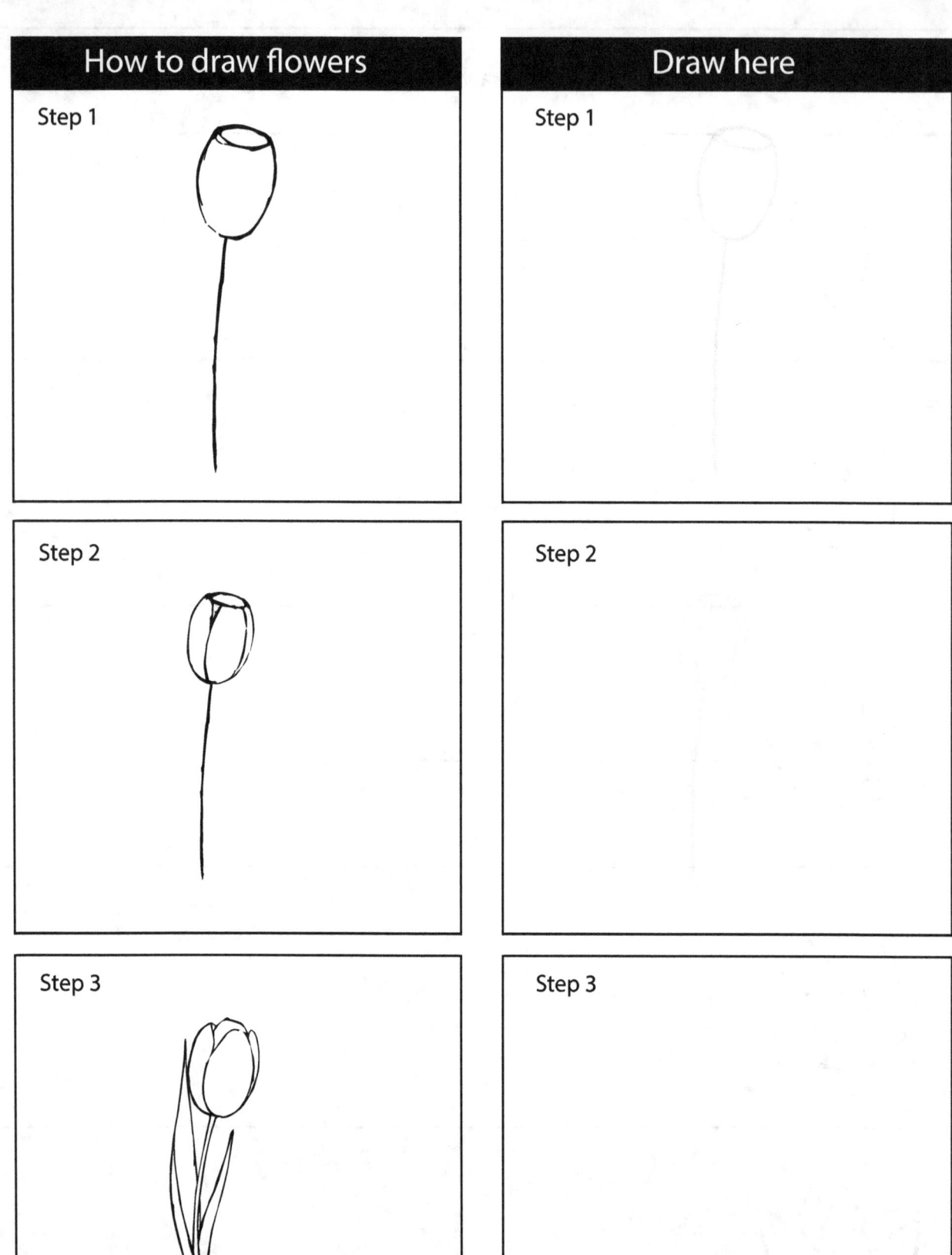

How to draw flowers

Step 1

Step 2

Step 3

Draw here

Step 1

Step 2

Step 3

How to draw flowers

Draw here

Step 1

Step 1

Step 2

Step 2

Step 3

Step 3

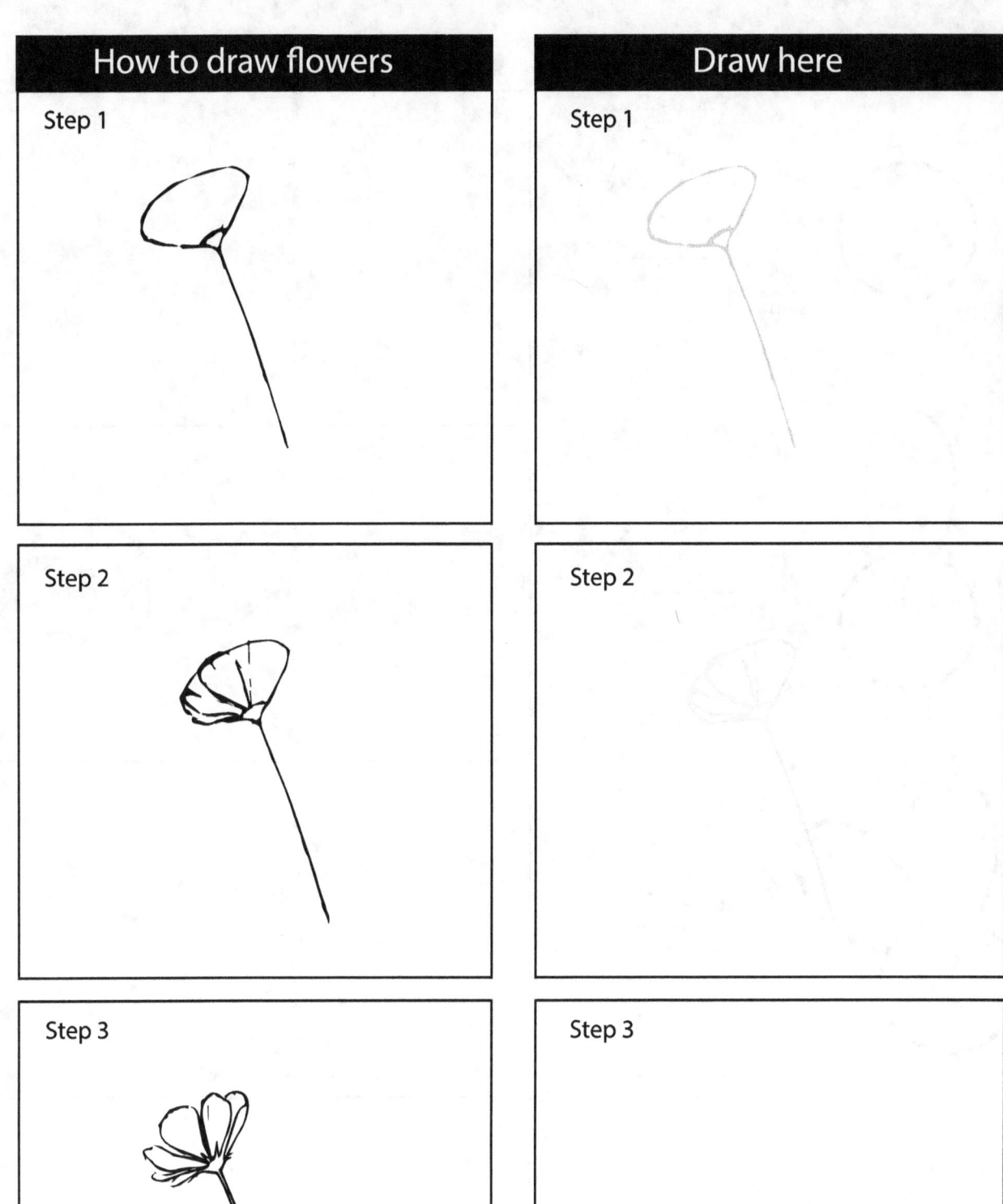

The Steps

Draw the Following Steps

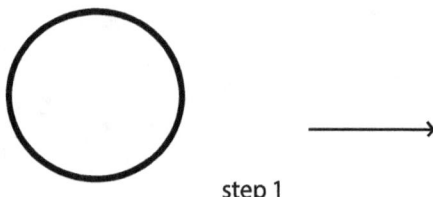

step 1

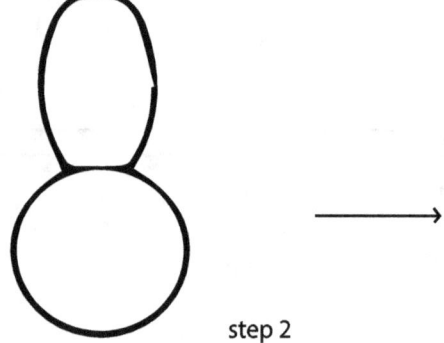

step 2

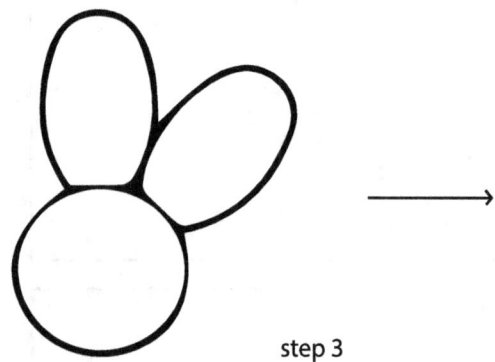

step 3

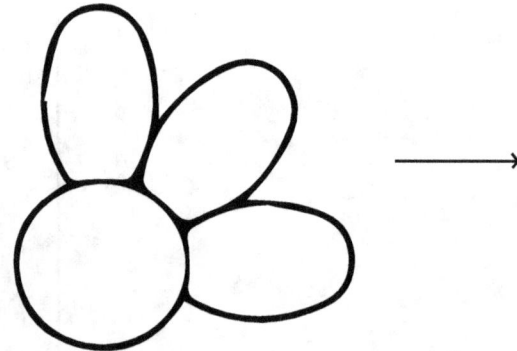

The Steps

Draw the Following Steps

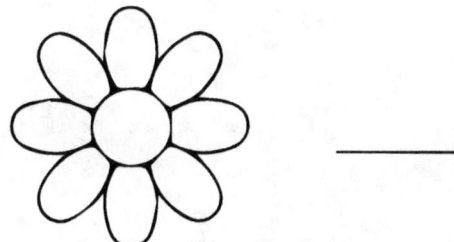

step 5

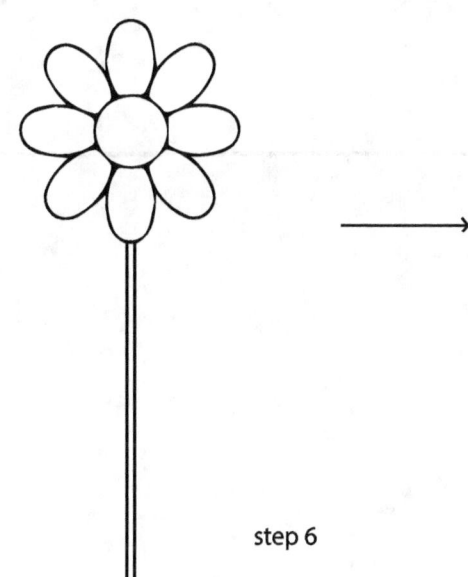

step 6

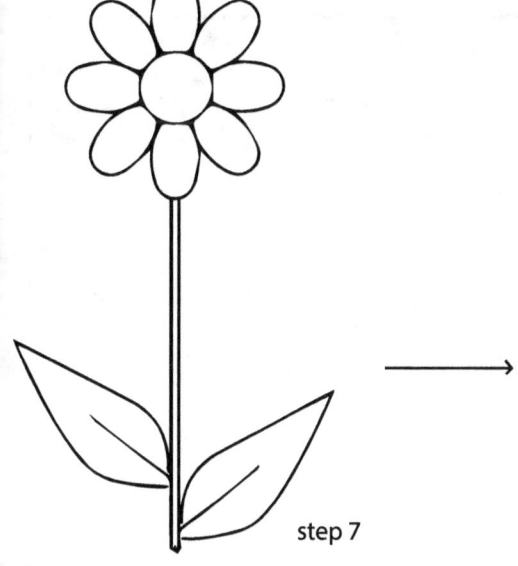

step 7

The Steps

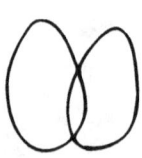

step 1

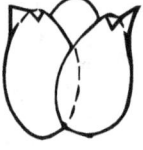

step 2

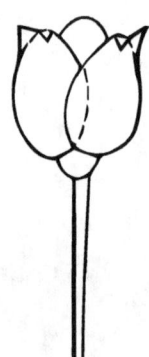

step 3

The Steps

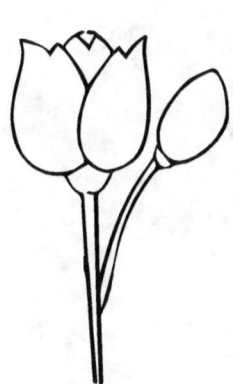

step 4

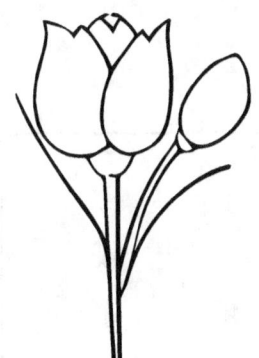

step 5

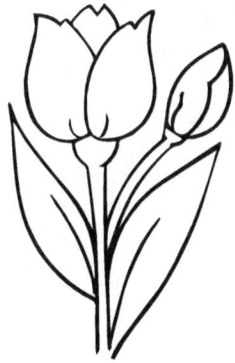

step 6

The Steps

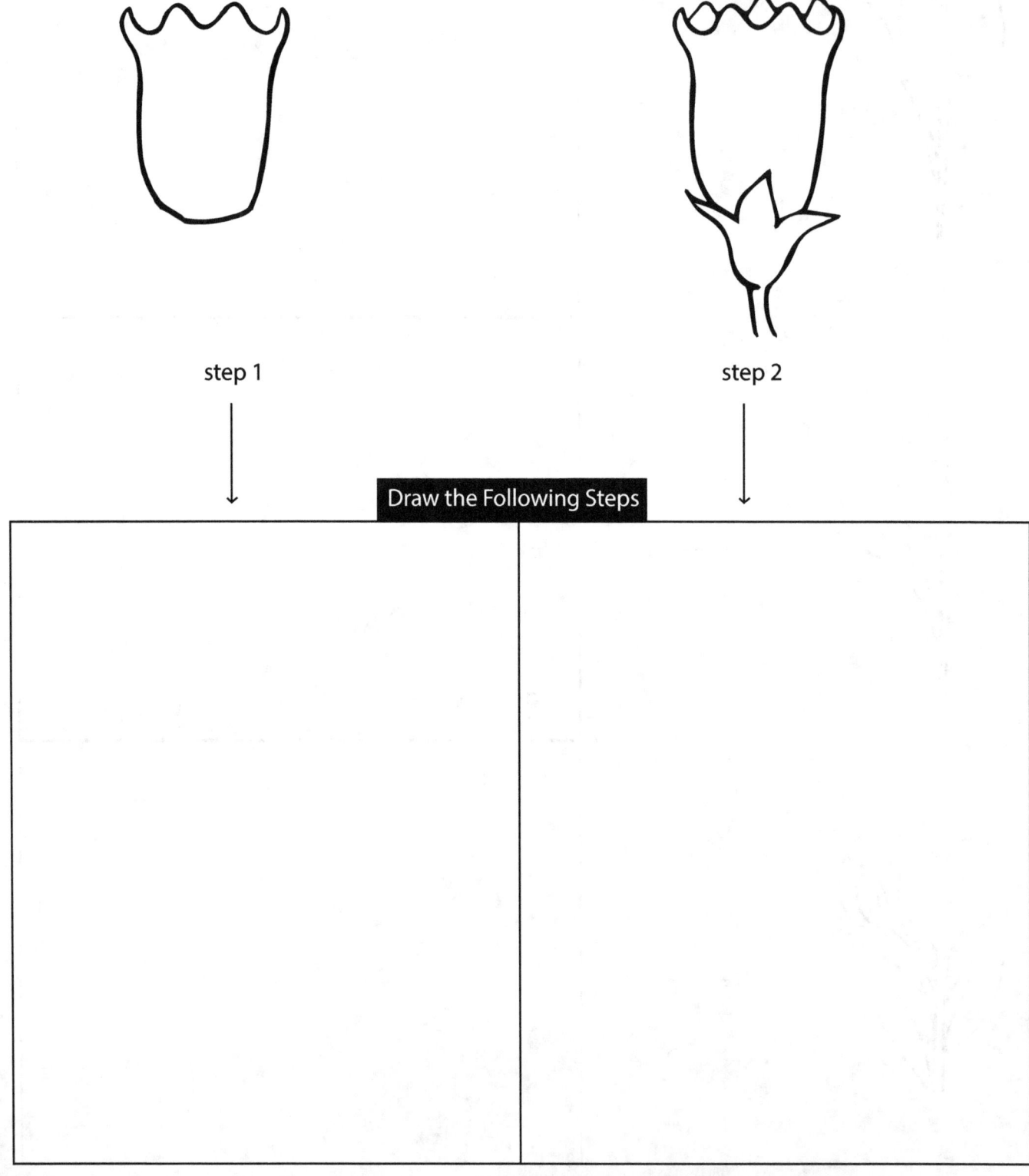

step 1

step 2

Draw the Following Steps

The Steps

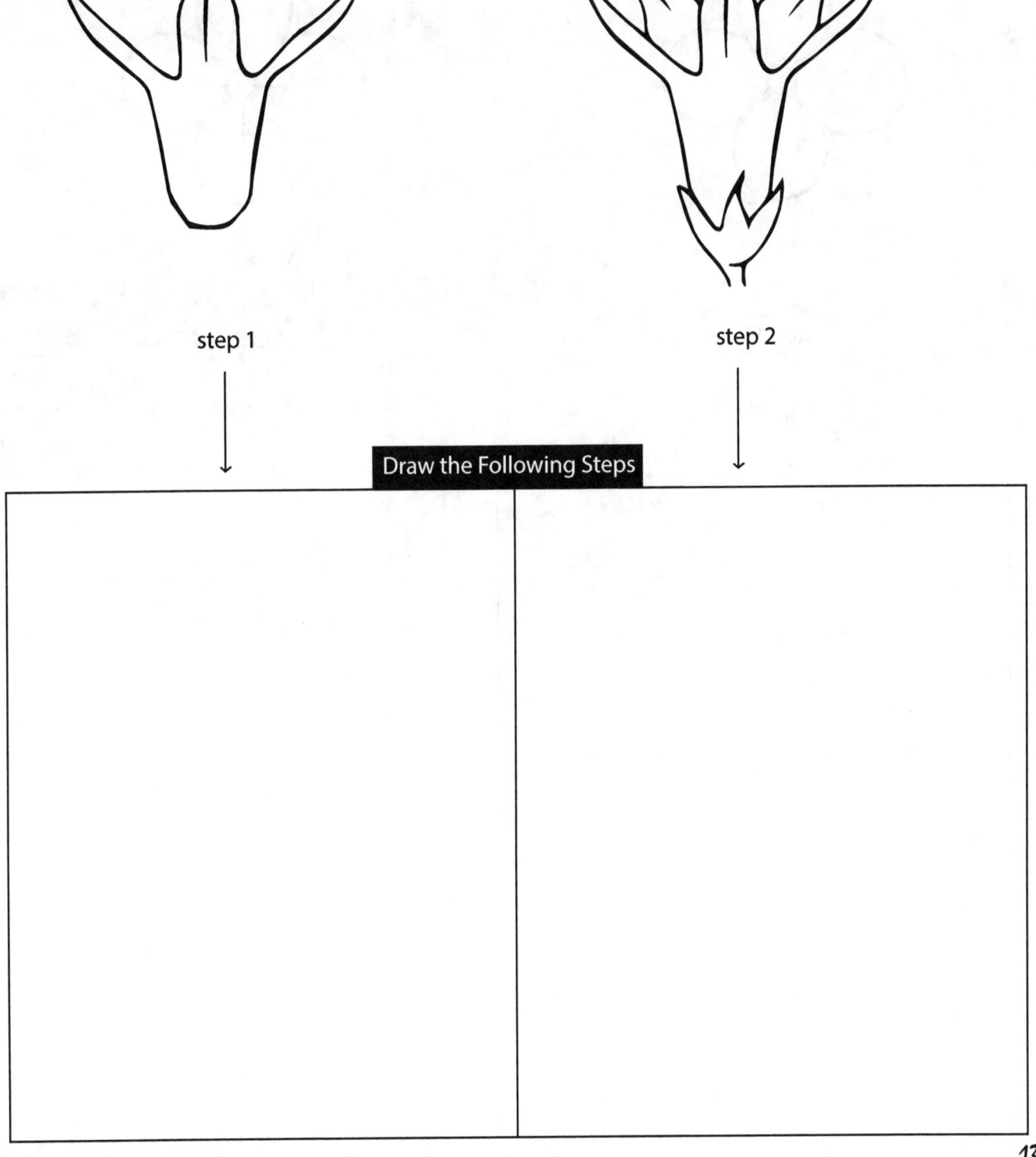

step 1

step 2

Draw the Following Steps

The Steps

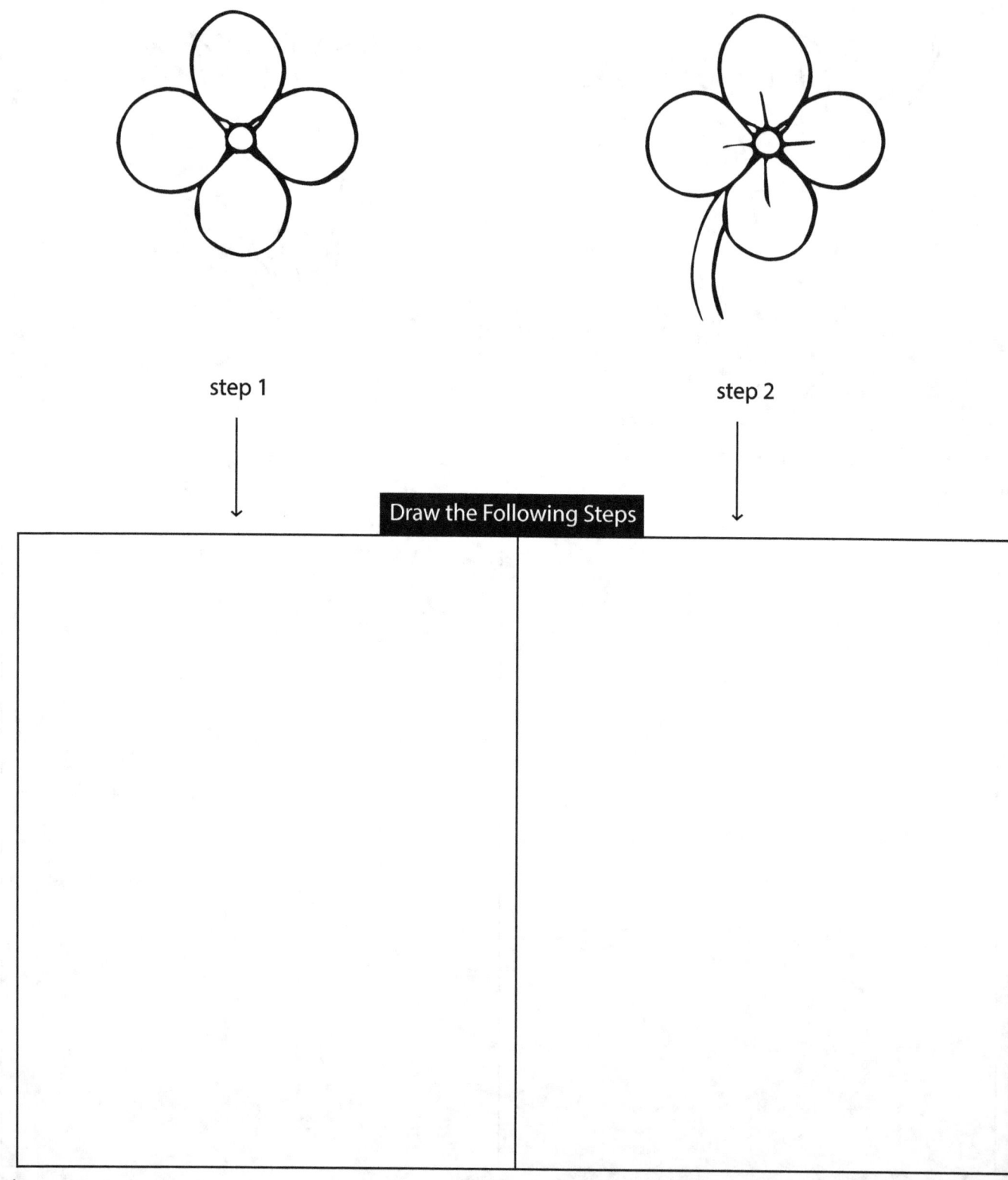

step 1

step 2

Draw the Following Steps

The Steps

Draw the Following Steps

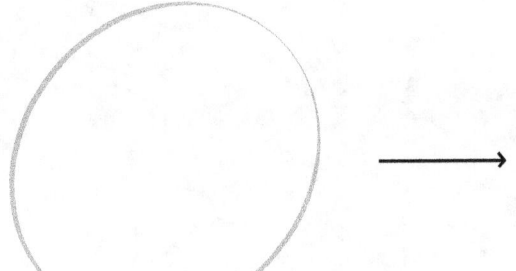

step 1

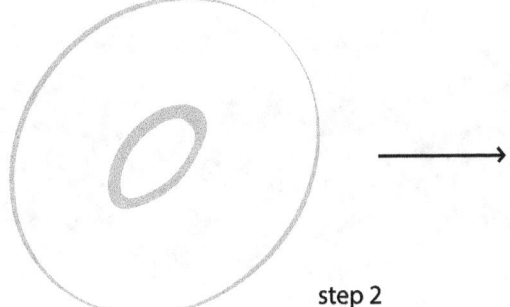

step 2

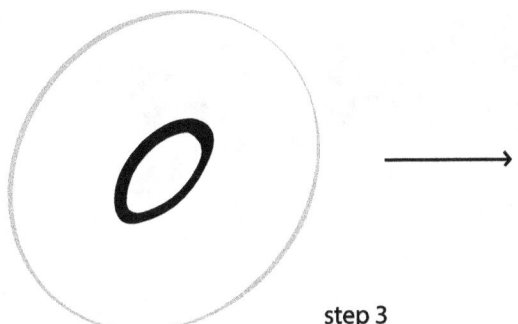

step 3

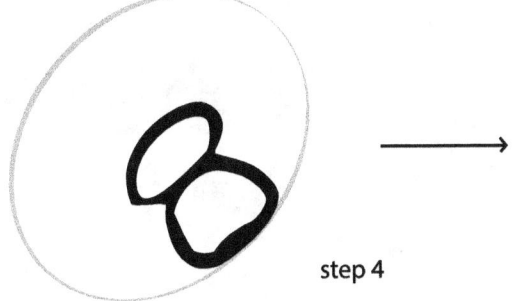

step 4

The Steps

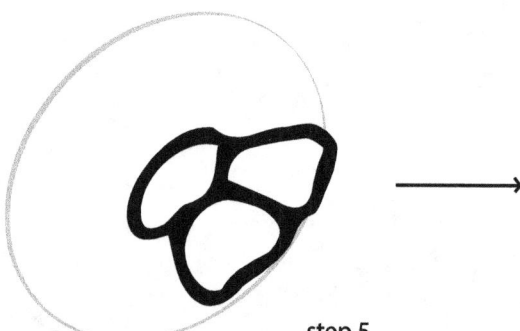

step 5

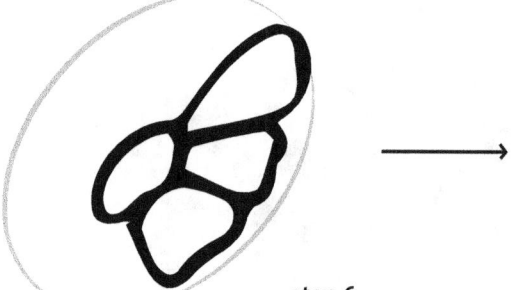

step 6

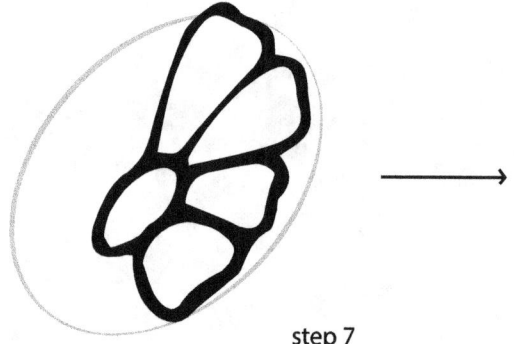

step 7

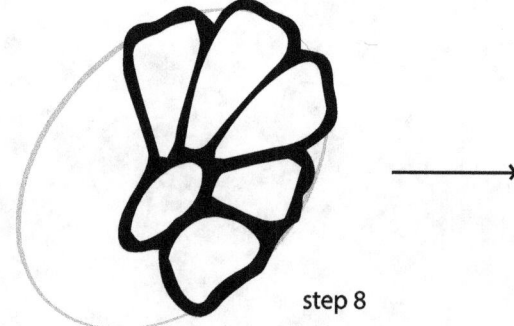

step 8

The Steps

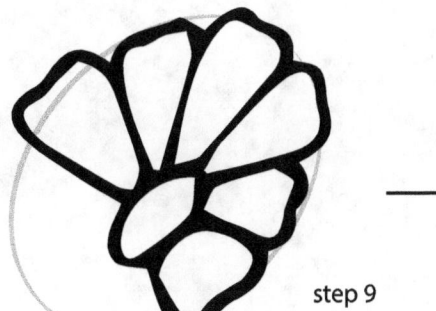

step 9

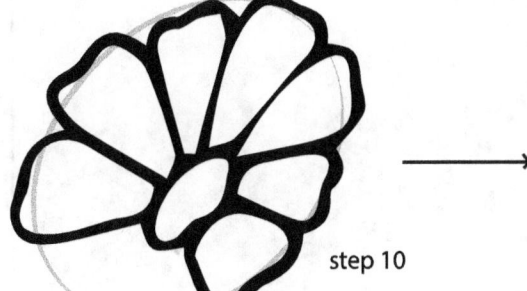

step 10

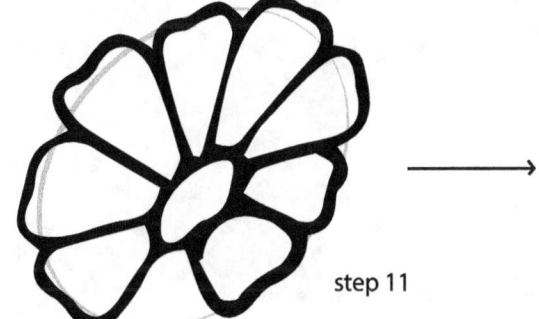

step 11

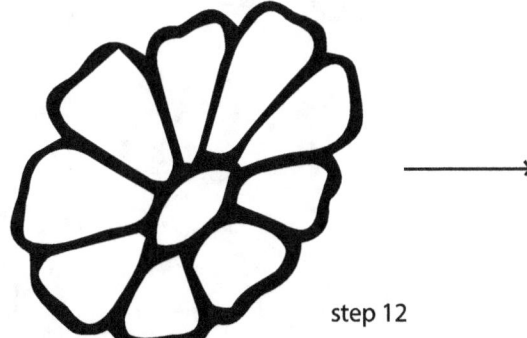

step 12

The Steps

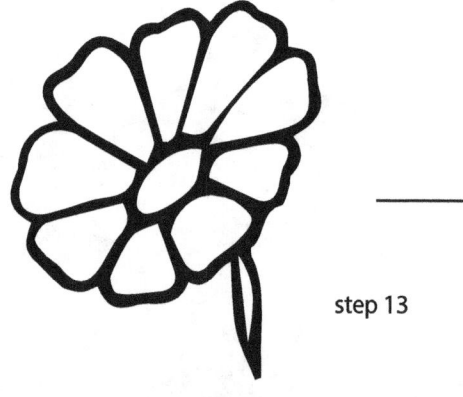

step 13

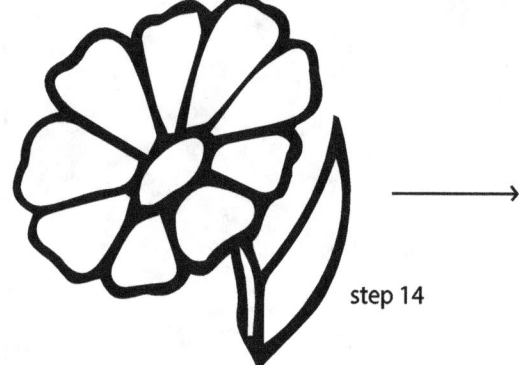

step 14

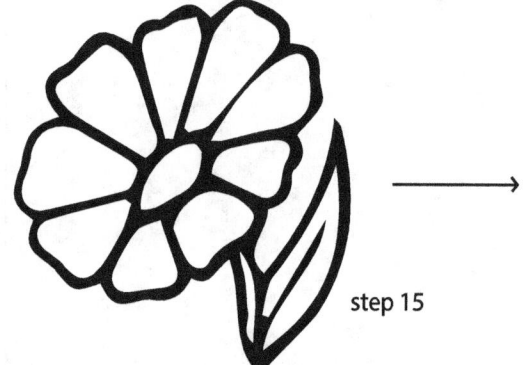

step 15

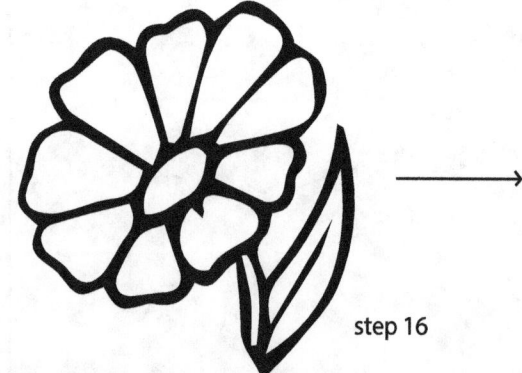

step 16

DRAWING TUTORIAL MOTH

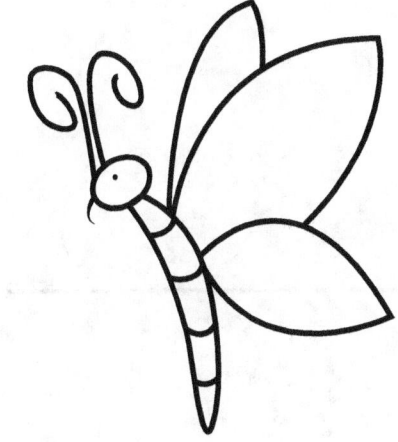
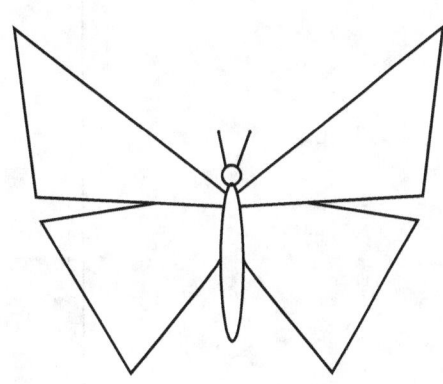
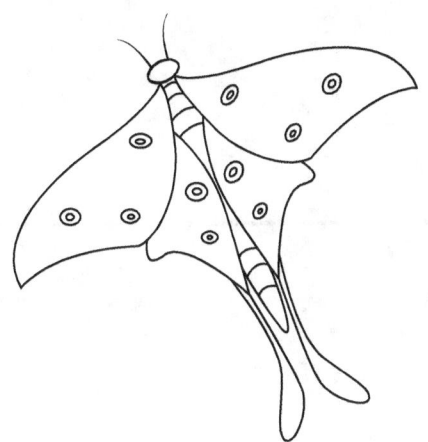
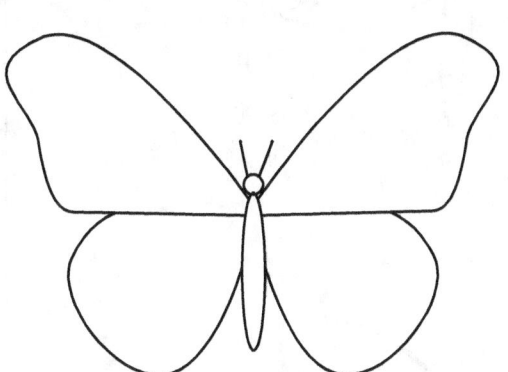

The Steps

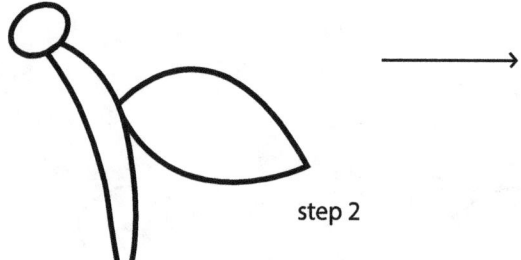

step 1

step 2

step 3

The Steps

Draw the Following Steps

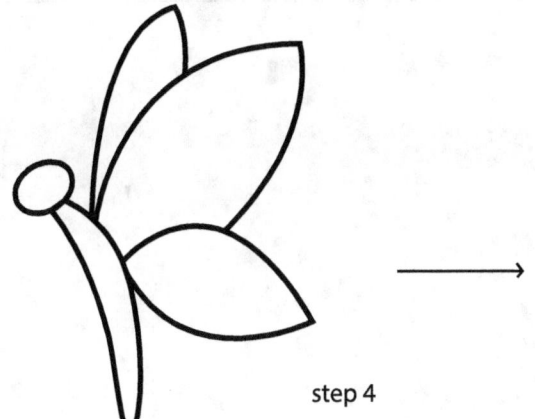

step 4

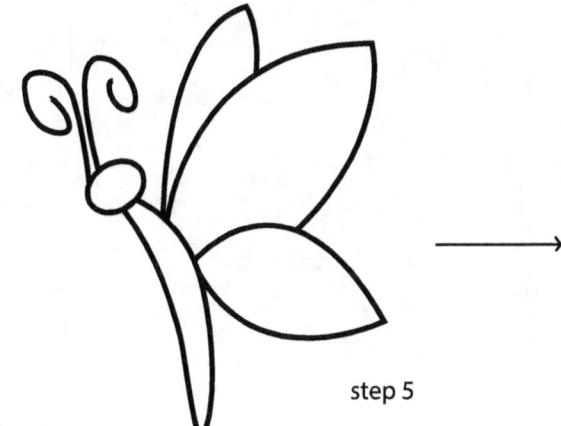

step 5

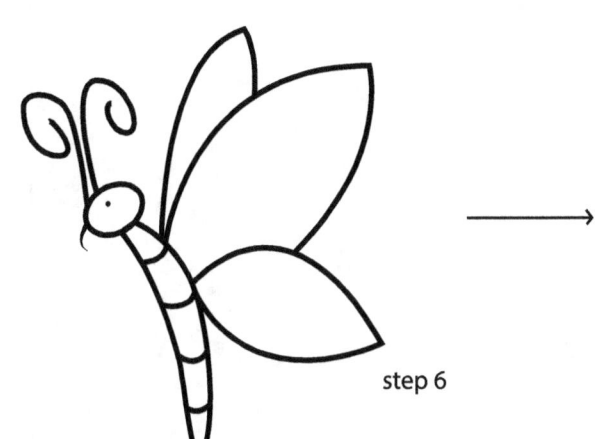

step 6

The Steps

Draw the Following Steps

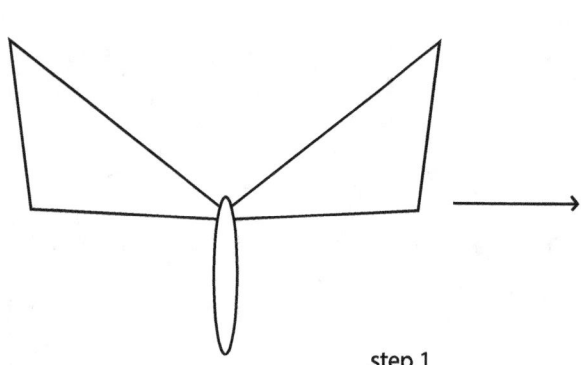

step 1

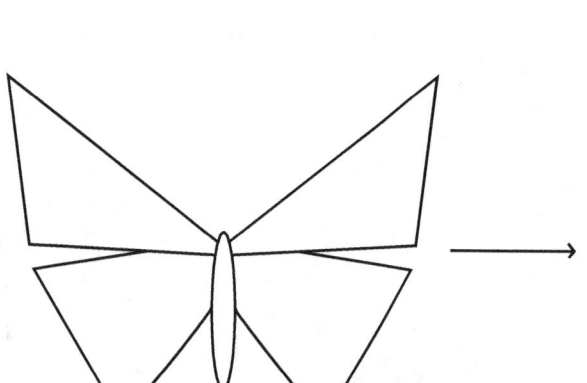

step 2

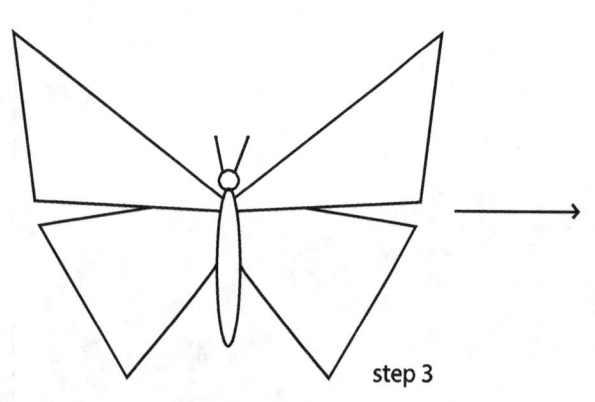

step 3

The Steps

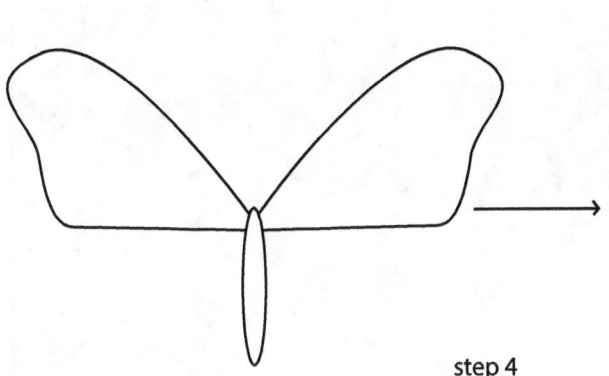

step 4

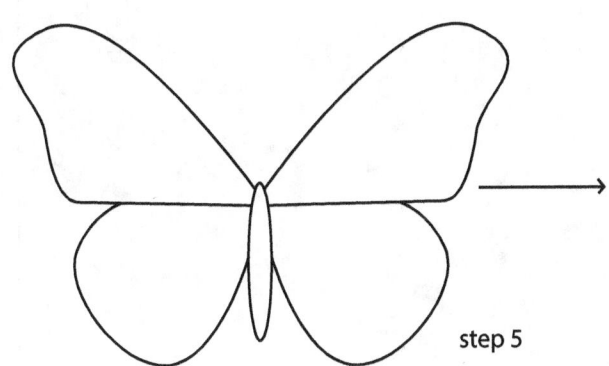

step 5

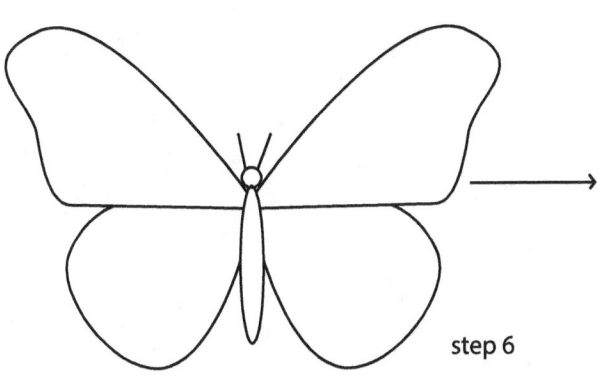

step 6

The Steps

Draw the Following Steps

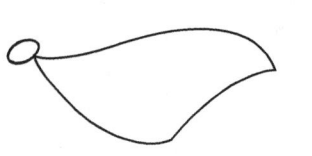

step 1

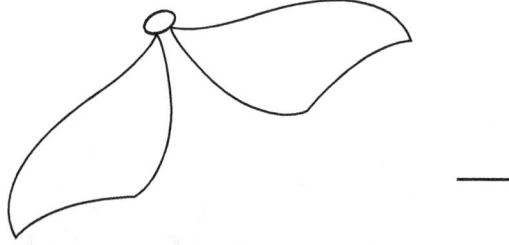

step 2

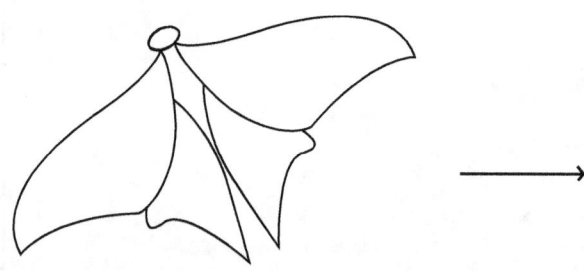

step 3

The Steps

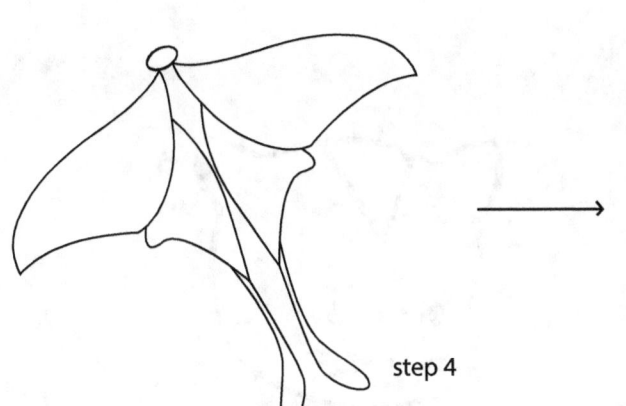

step 4

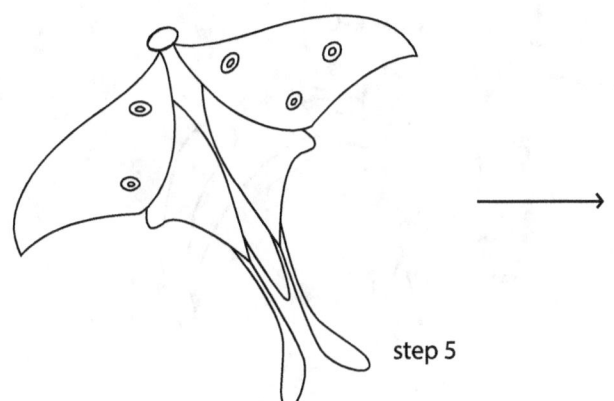

step 5

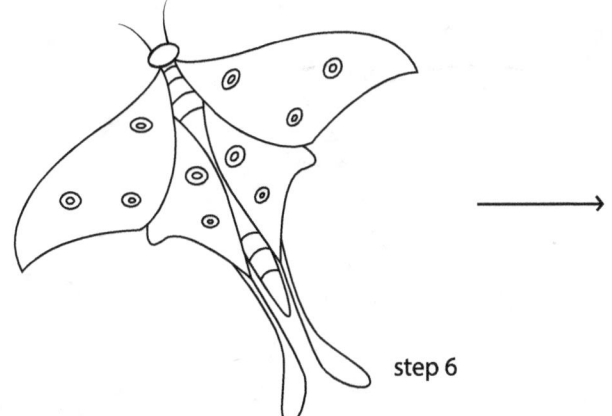

step 6

DRAWING TUTORIAL CATS

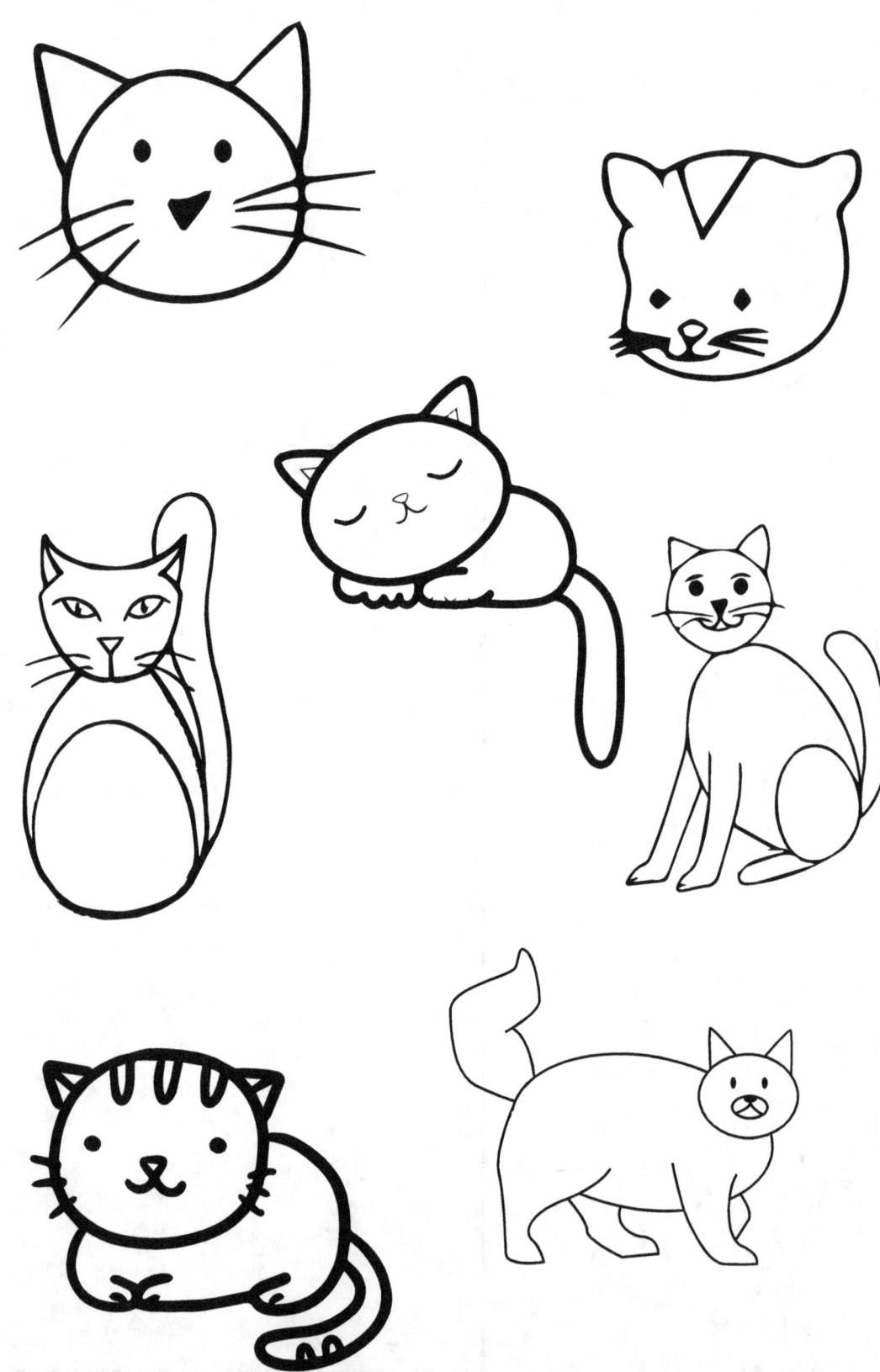

The Steps

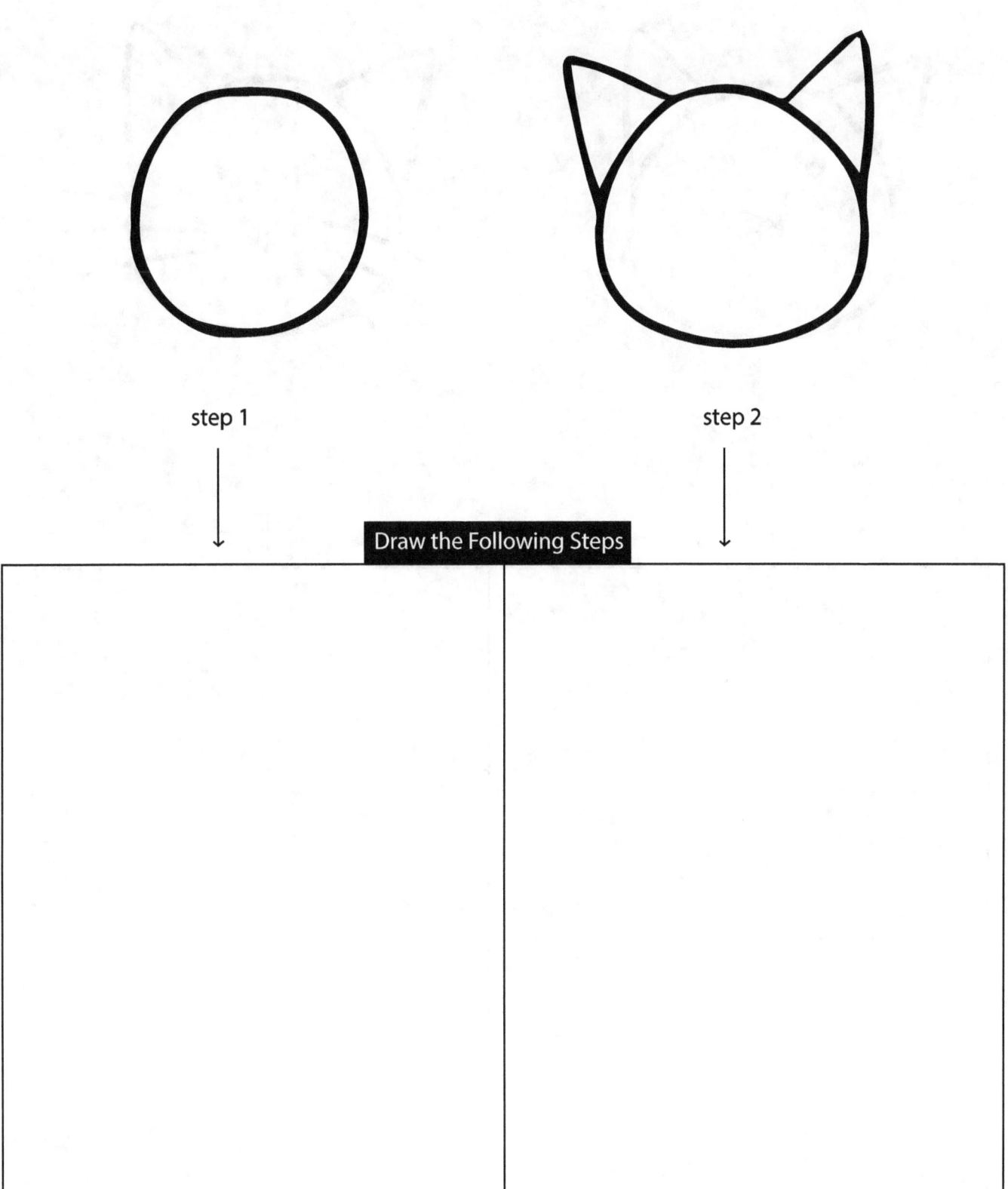

step 1

step 2

Draw the Following Steps

The Steps

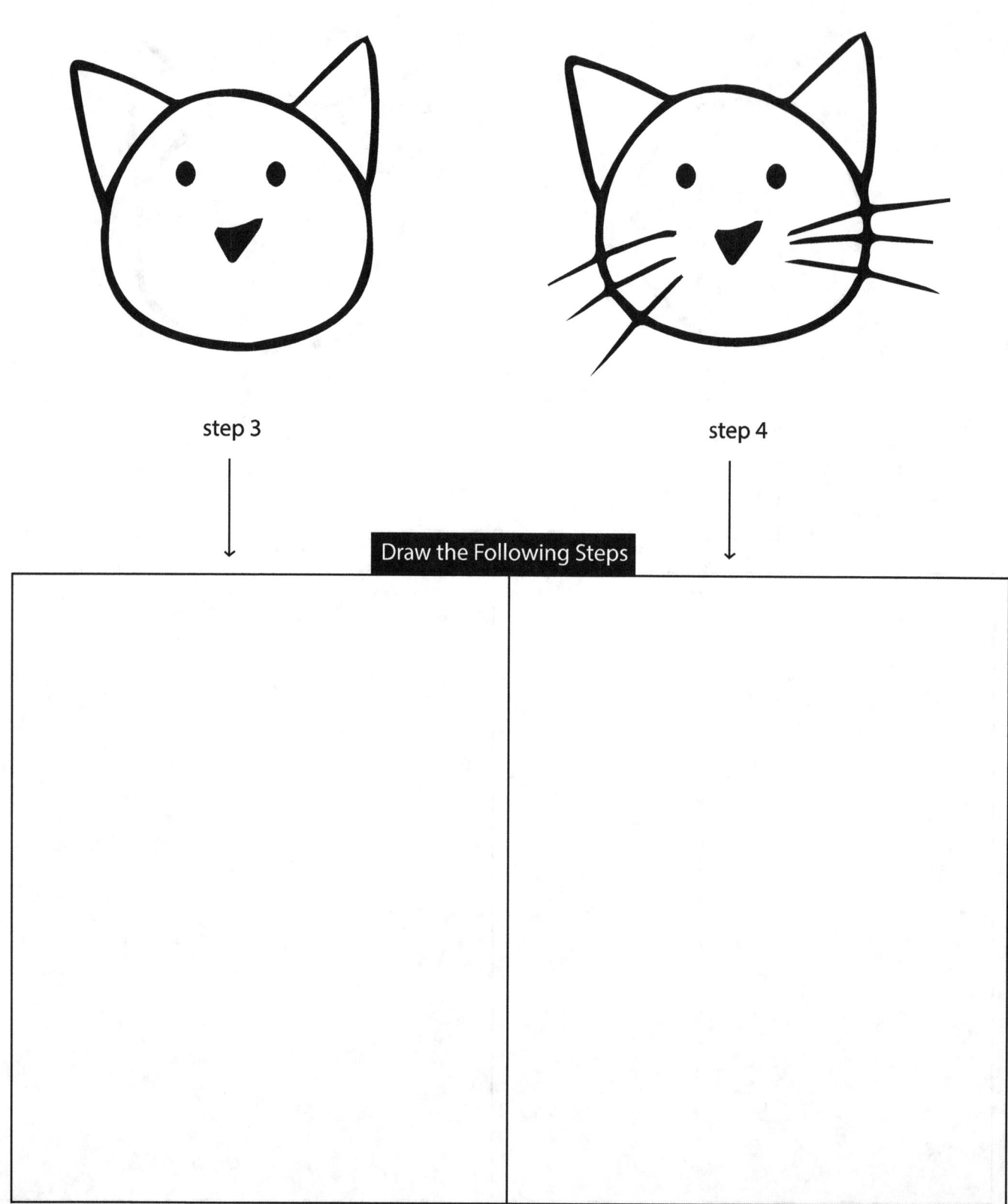

step 3

step 4

Draw the Following Steps

28

The Steps

Draw the Following Steps

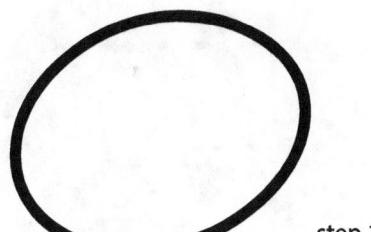

step 1

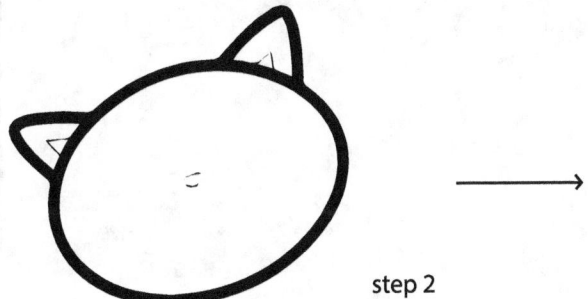

step 2

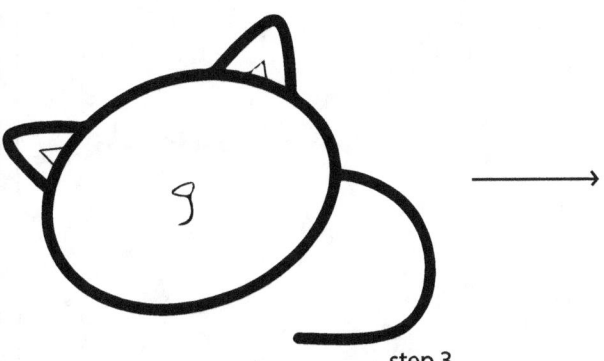

step 3

The Steps

Draw the Following Steps

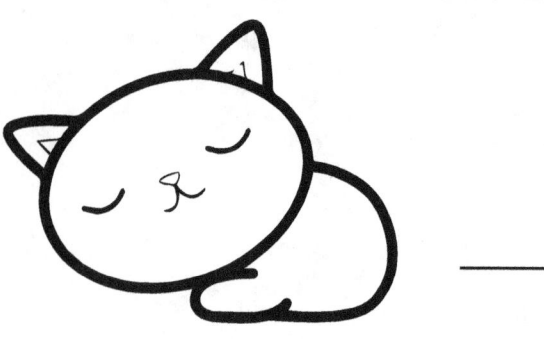

step 4

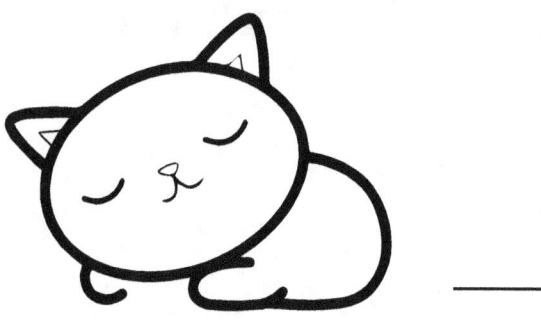

step 5

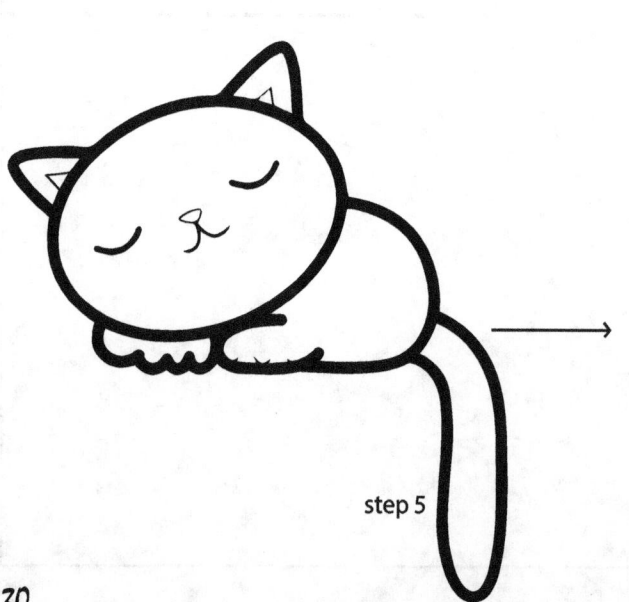

step 5

The Steps

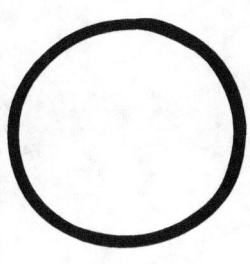

step 1

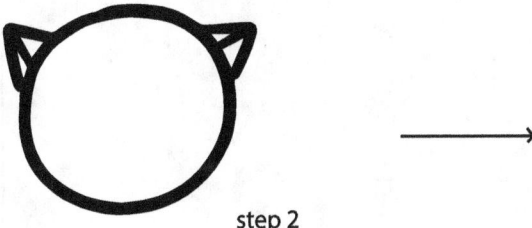

step 2

step 3

The Steps

Draw the Following Steps

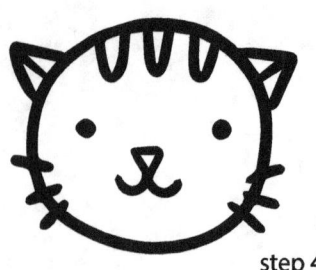

step 4

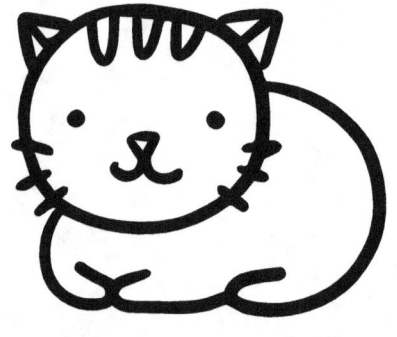

step 5

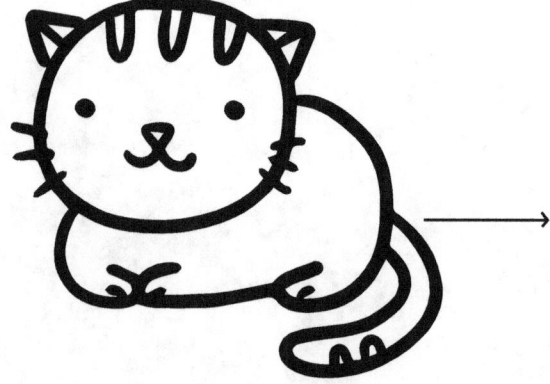

step 6

The Steps

→ step 1

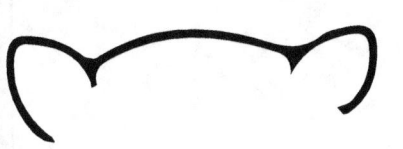

→ step 2

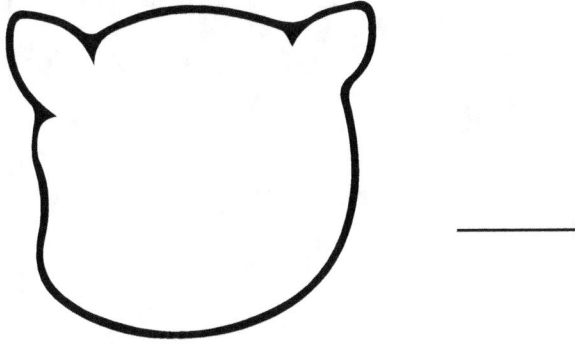

→ step 3

The Steps

Draw the Following Steps

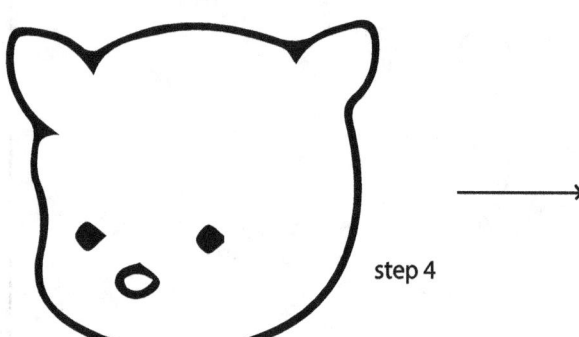

step 4

step 5

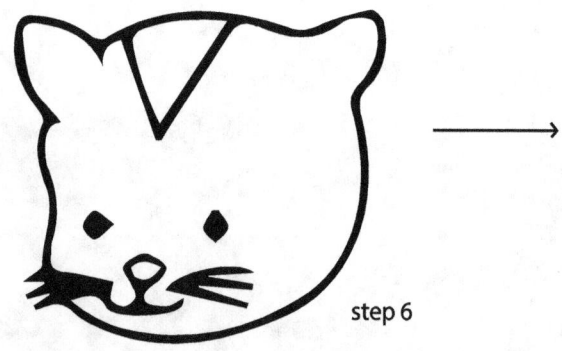

step 6

The Steps

Draw the Following Steps

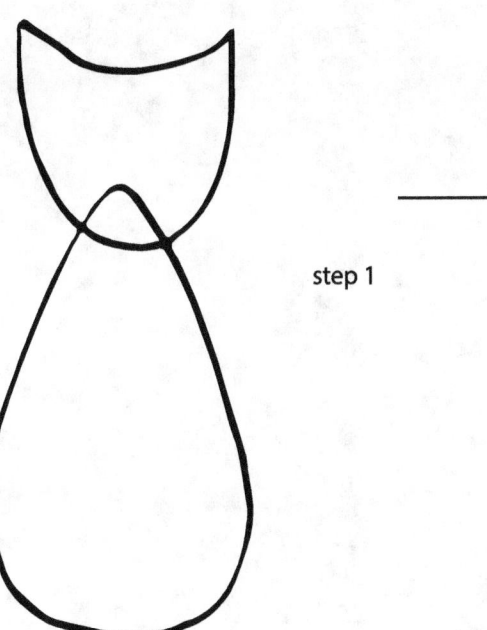

step 1

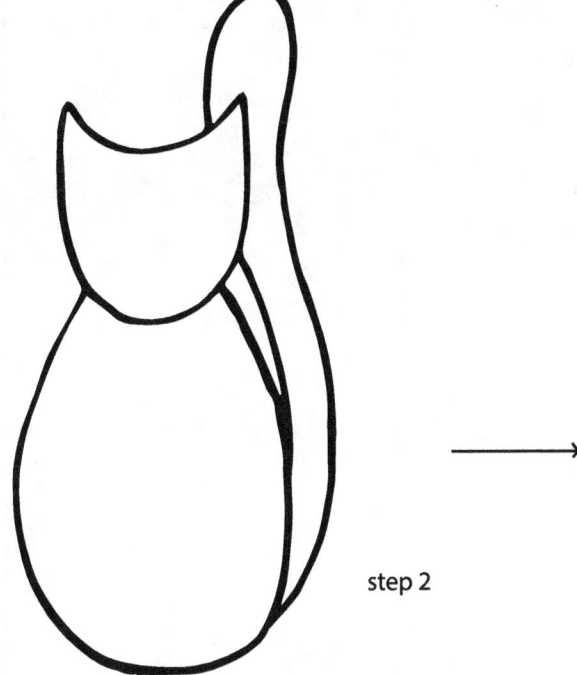

step 2

35

The Steps

Draw the Following Steps

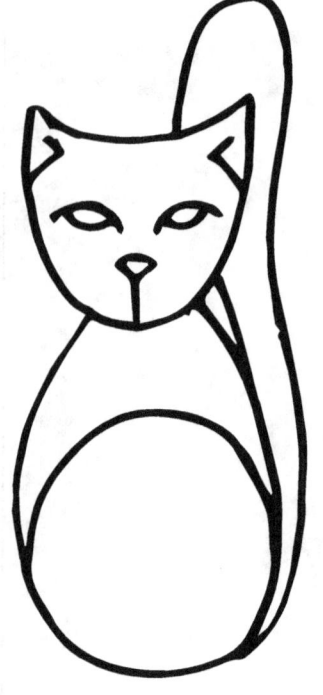

step 3

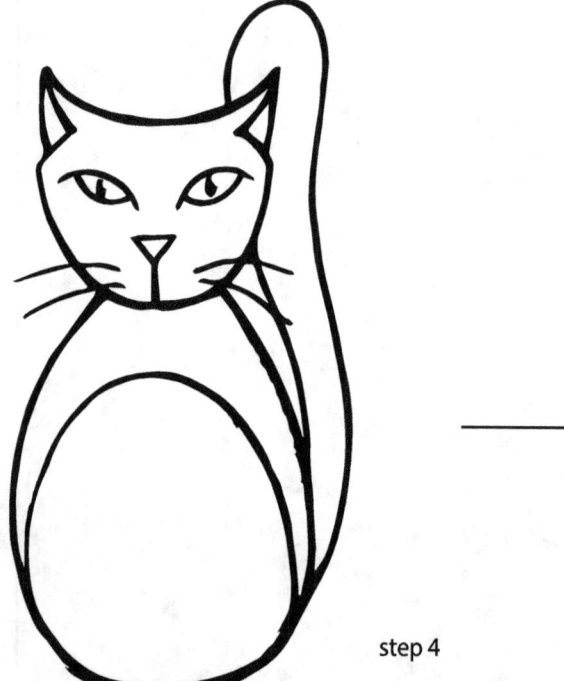

step 4

36

The Steps

Draw the Following Steps

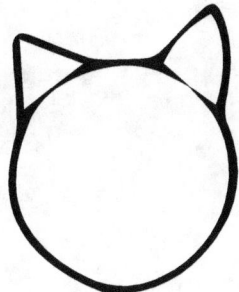

step 1

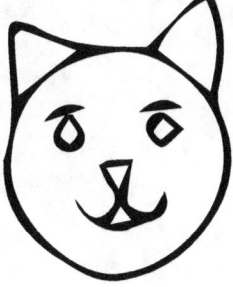

step 2

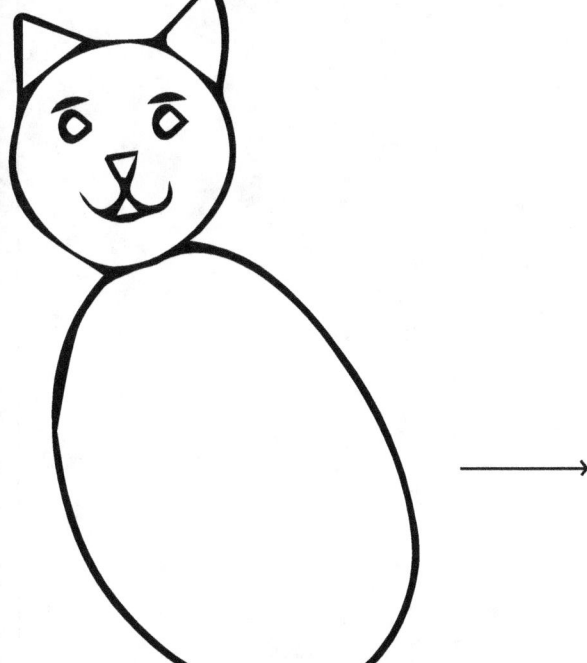

step 3

The Steps

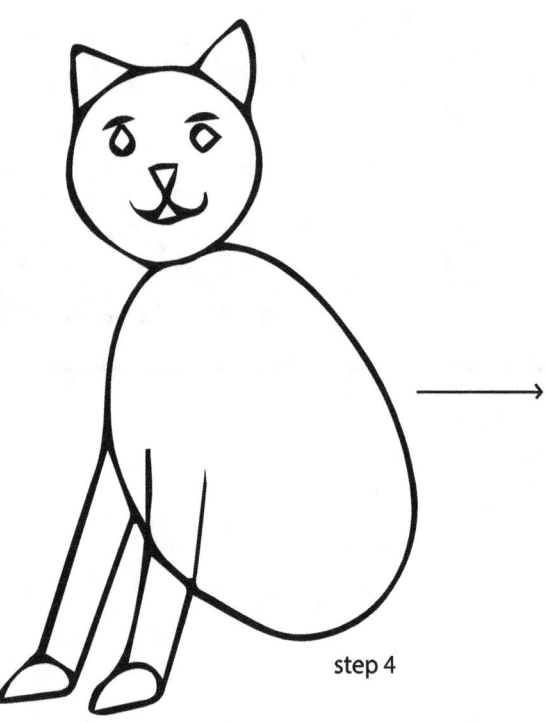

step 4

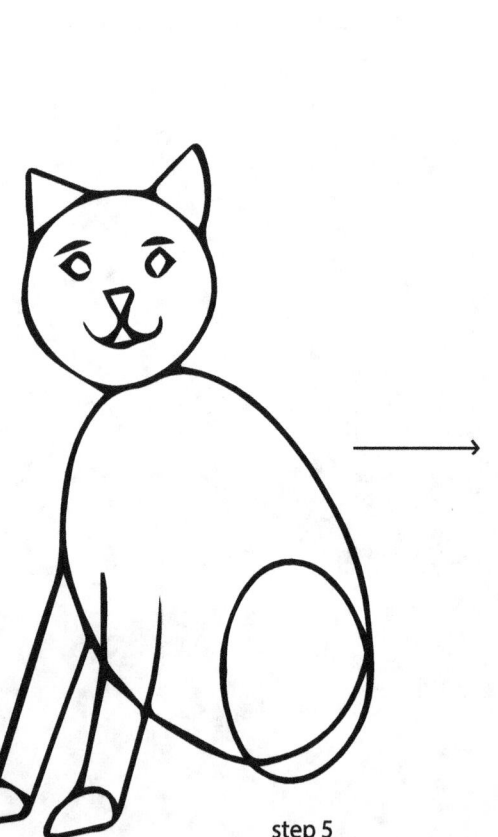

step 5

The Steps

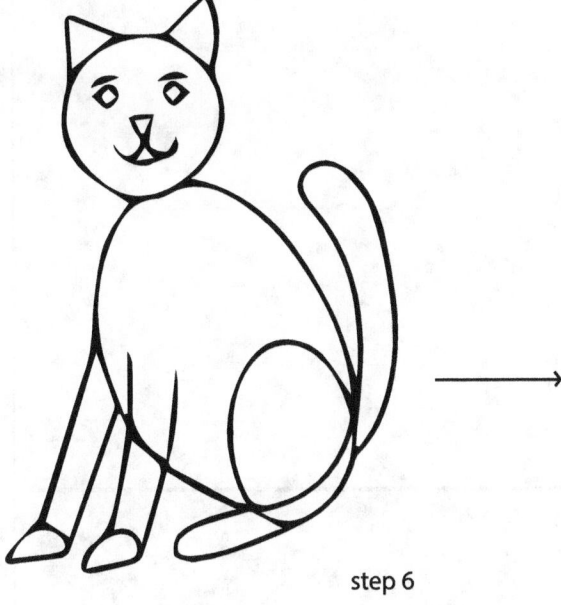

step 6

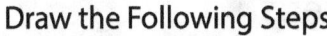

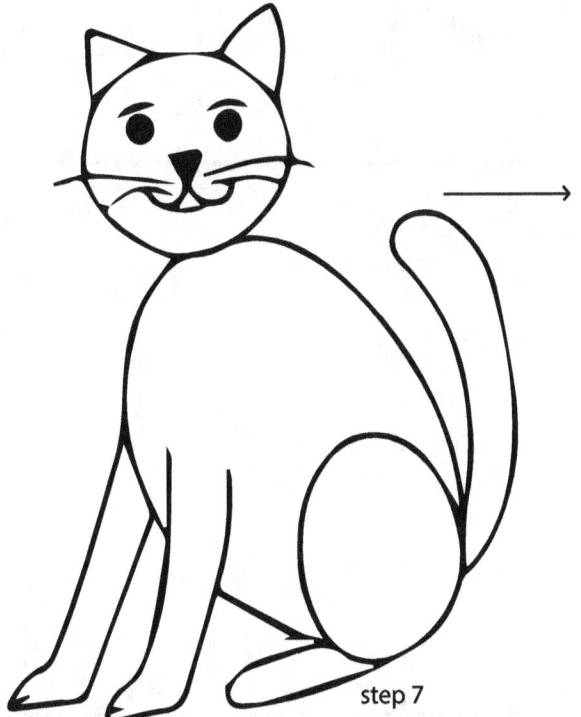

step 7

The Steps

Draw the Following Steps

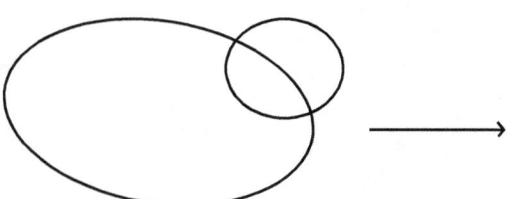

step 1

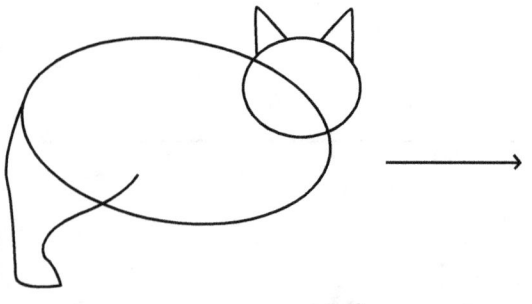

step 2

step 3

The Steps

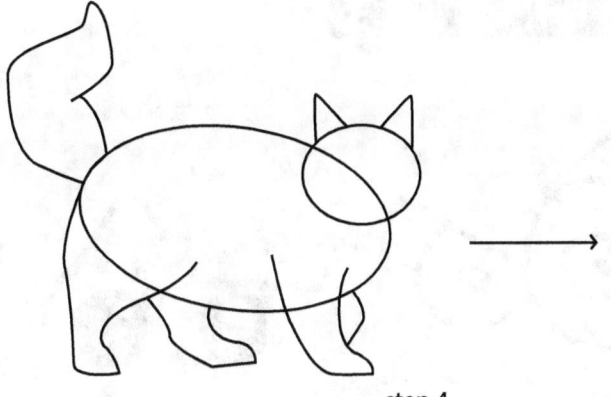

step 4

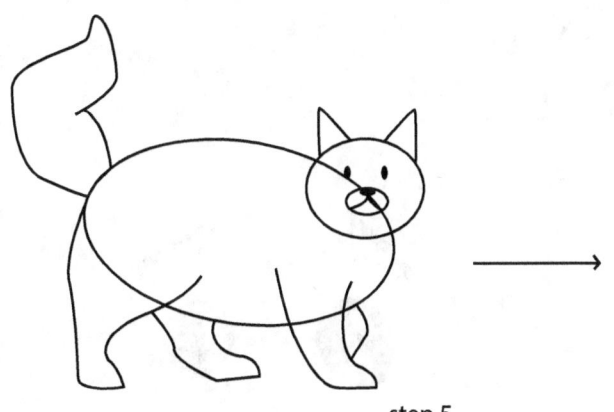

step 5

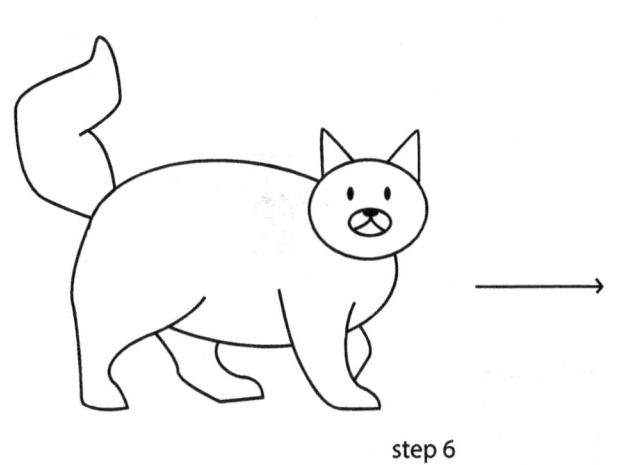

step 6

DRAWING TUTORIAL EYES

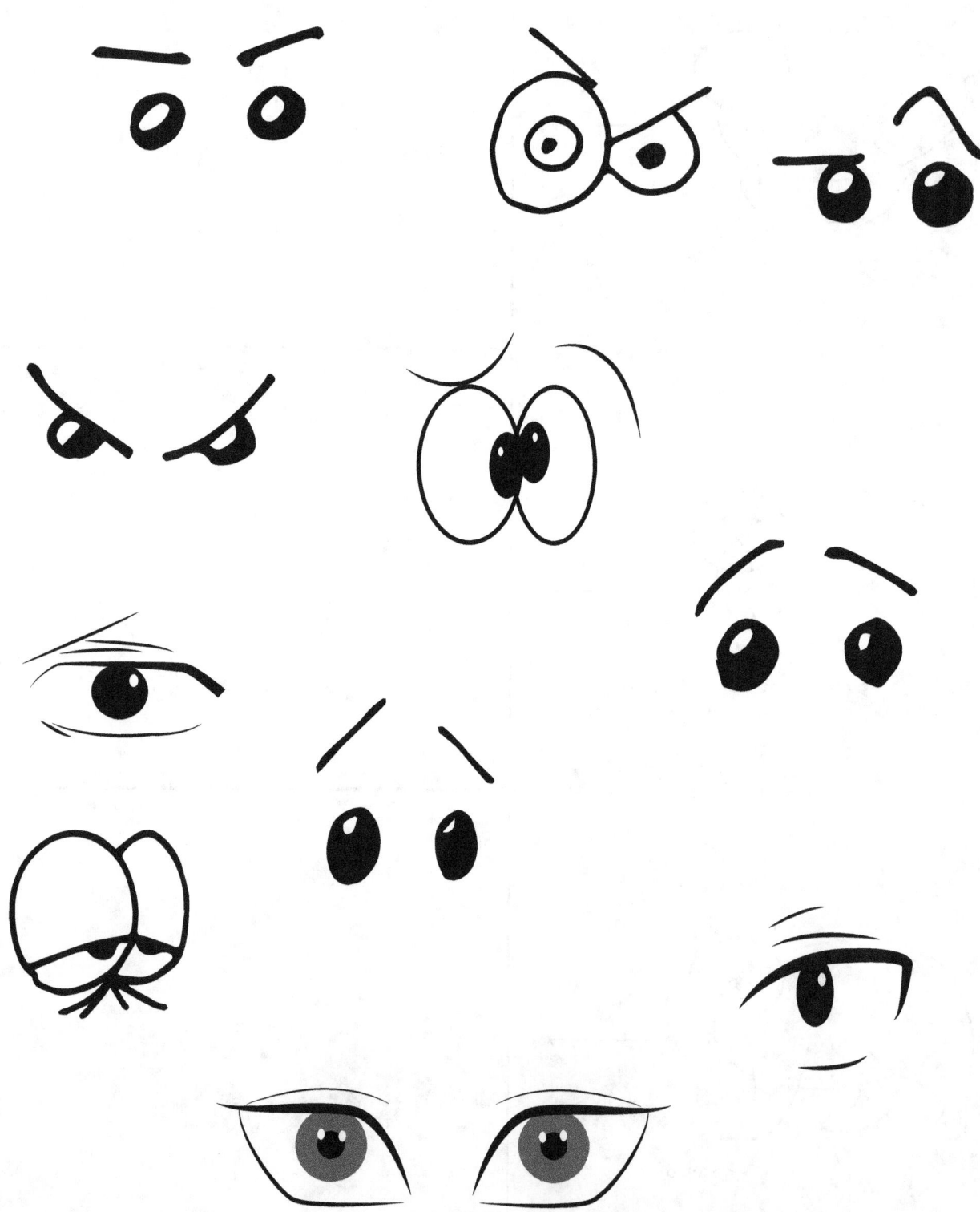

The Steps

Draw the Following Steps

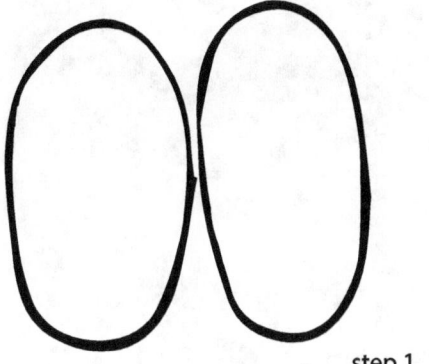

step 1

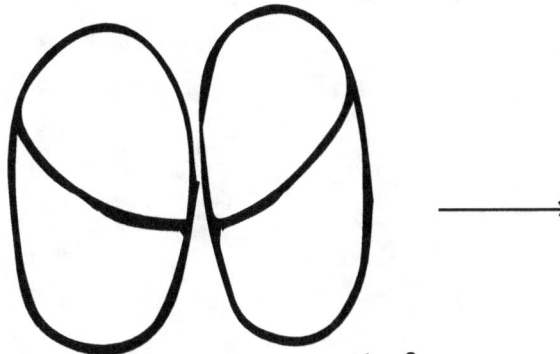

step 2

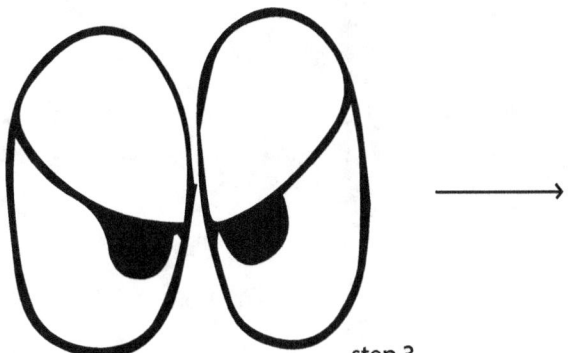

step 3

The Steps

Draw the Following Steps

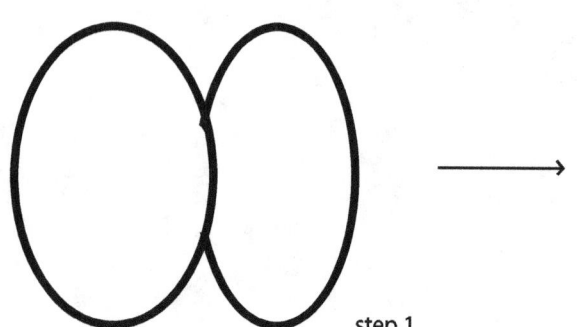

step 1

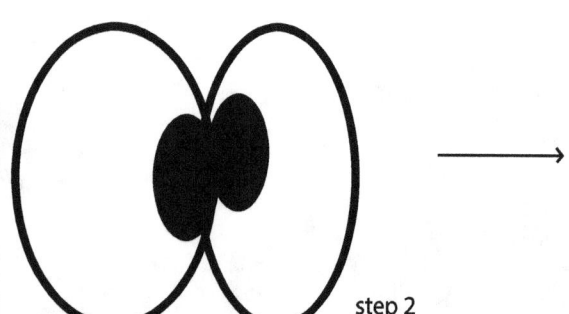

step 2

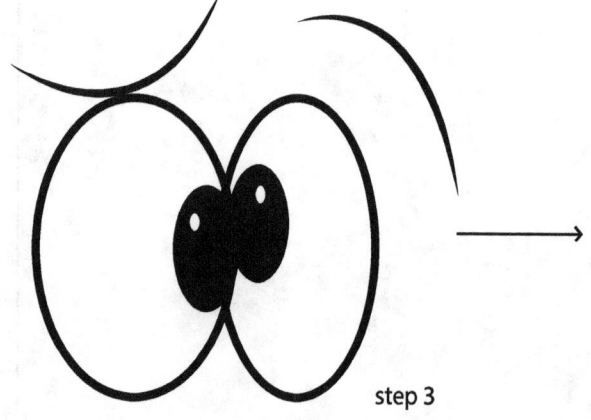

step 3

The Steps

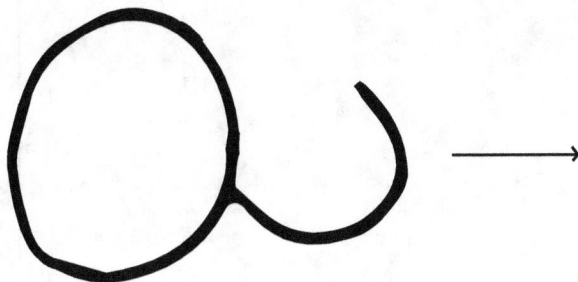

step 1

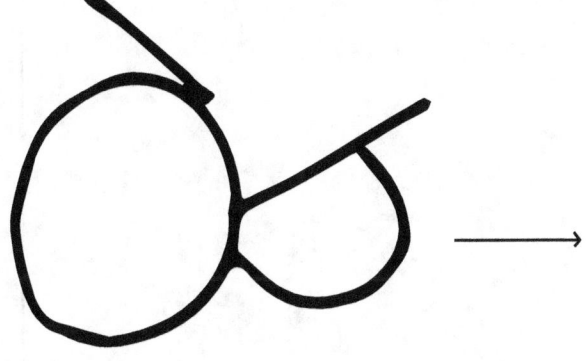

step 2

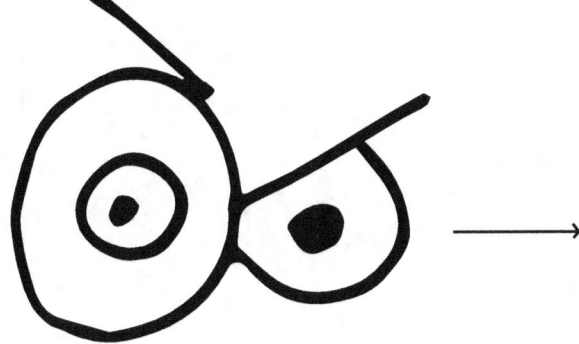

step 3

The Steps

step 1

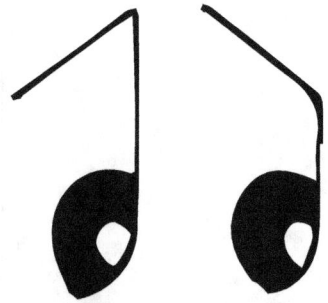

step 2

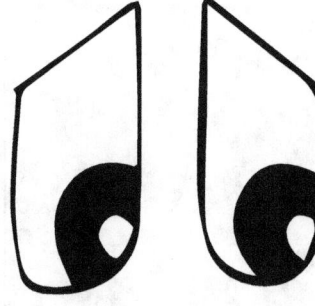

step 3

The Steps

step 1

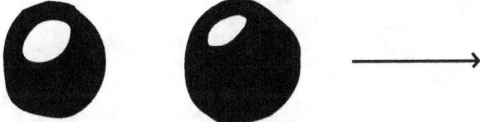

step 2

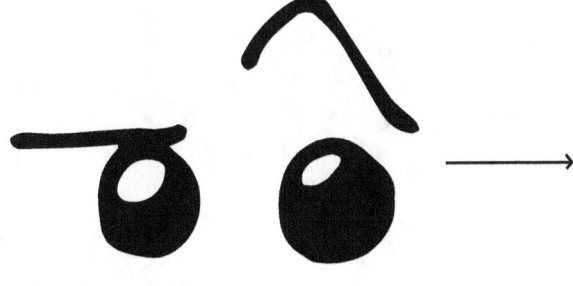

step 3

The Steps

  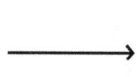

step 1

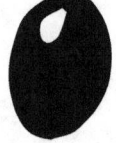 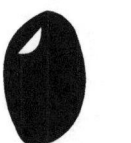

step 2

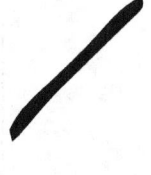  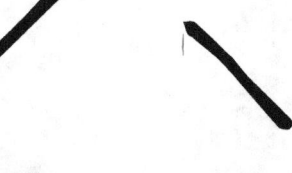

step 3

The Steps

Draw the Following Steps

 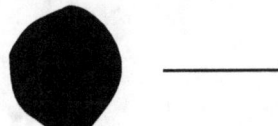

step 1

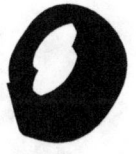 

step 2

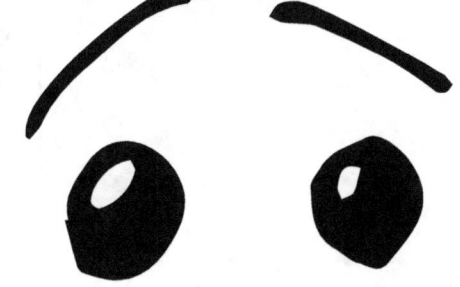

step 3

The Steps

Draw the Following Steps

step 1

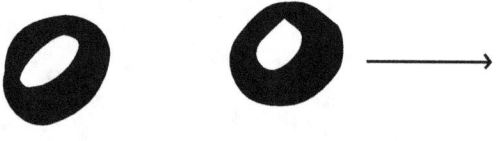

step 2

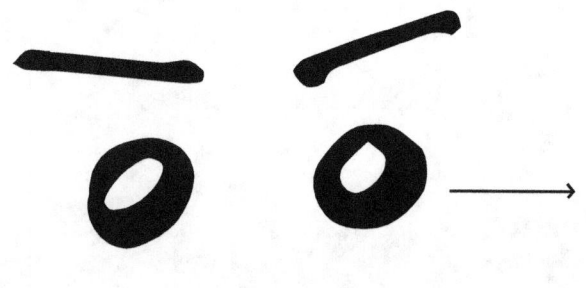

step 3

The Steps

Draw the Following Steps

step 1

step 2

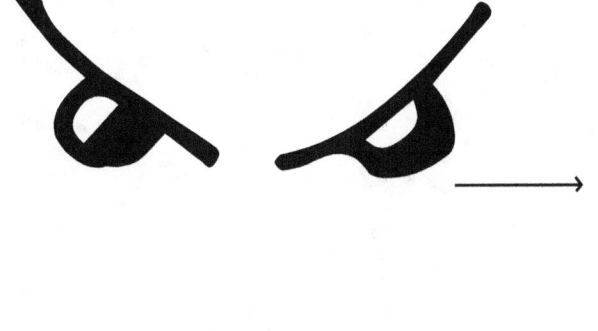

step 3

The Steps

Draw the Following Steps

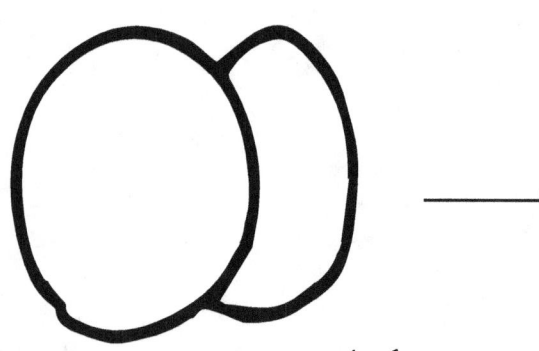

step 1

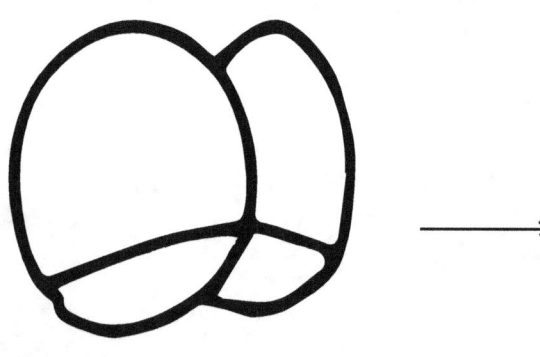

step 2

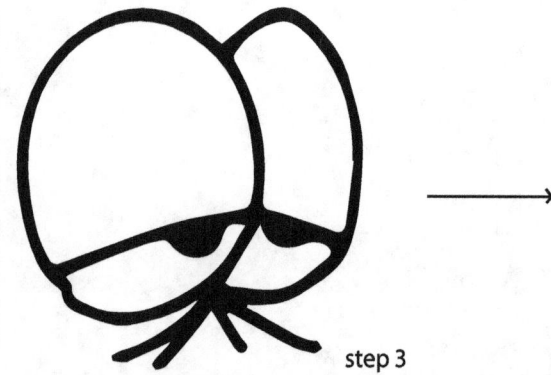

step 3

The Steps

Draw the Following Steps

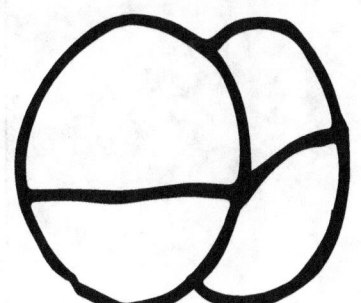

step 1

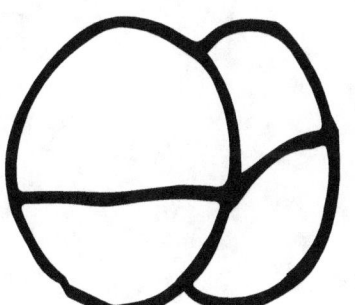

step 2

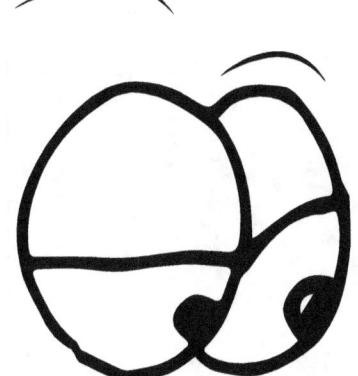

step 3

The Steps

Draw the Following Steps

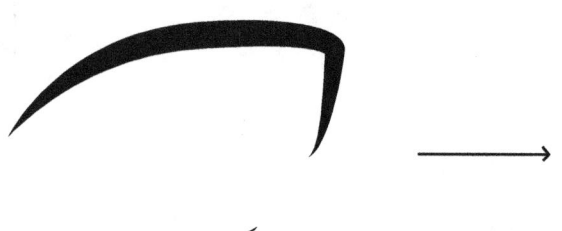

step 1

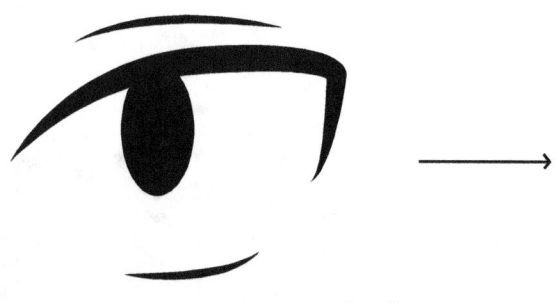

step 2

step 3

The Steps

Draw the Following Steps

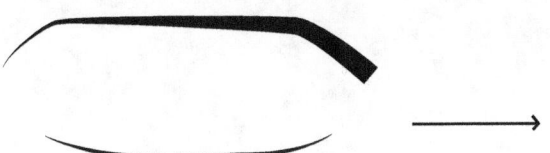

step 1

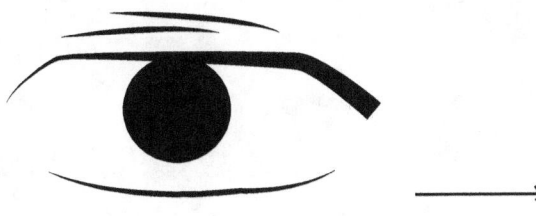

step 2

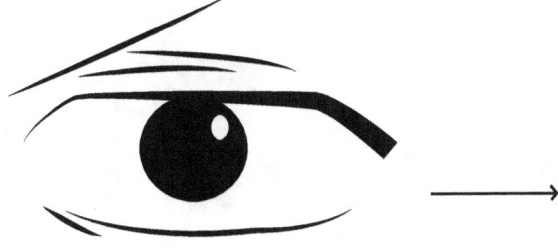

step 3

The Steps

Draw the Following Steps

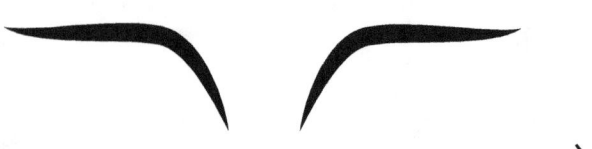

step 1

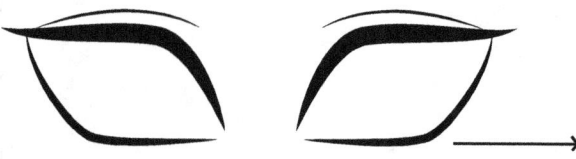

step 2

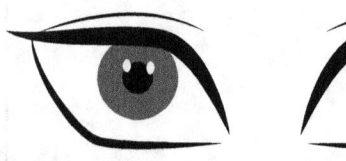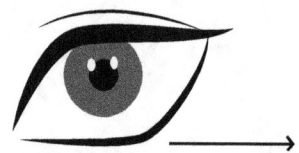

step 3

DRAWING TUTORIAL CARS

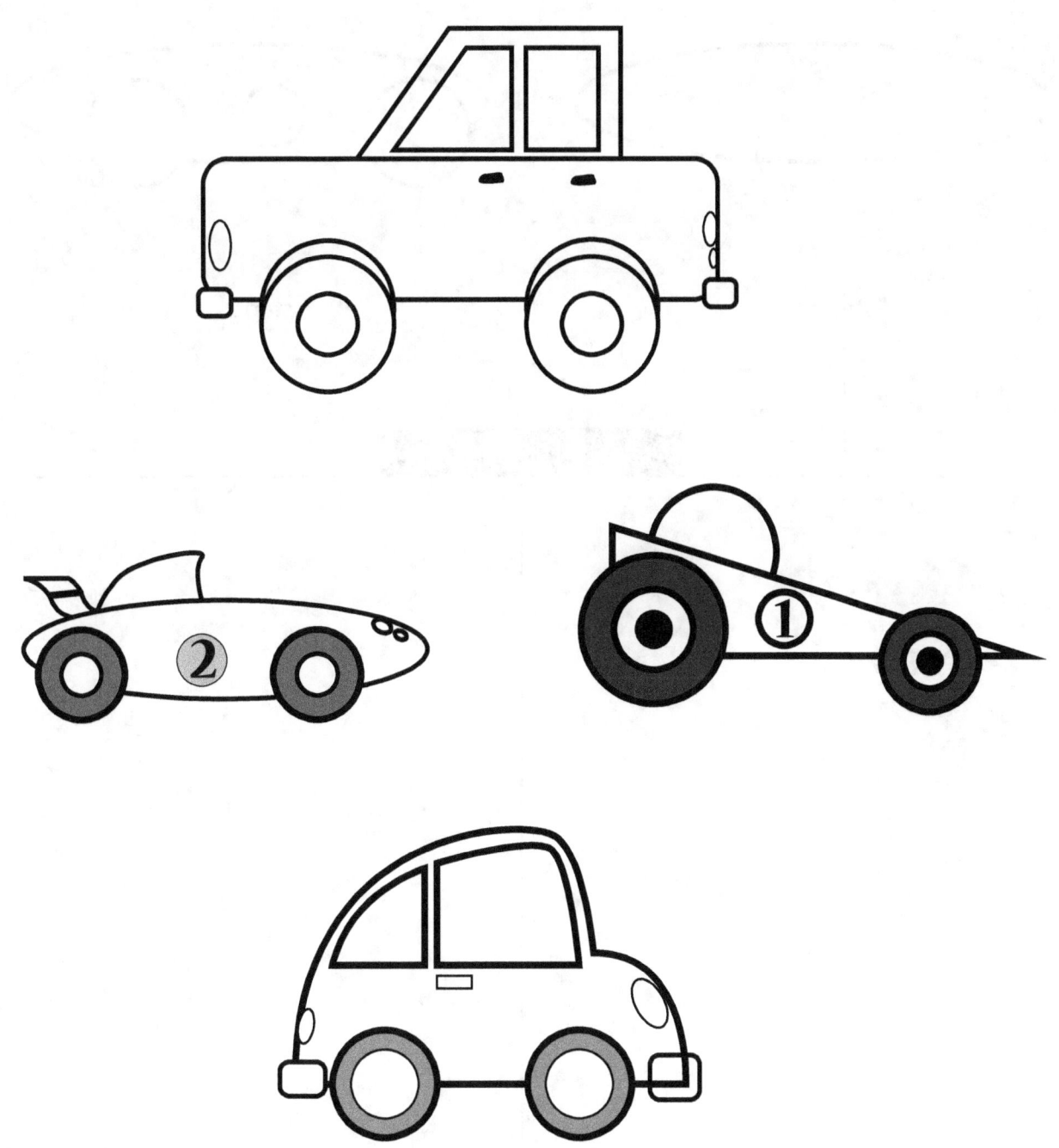

The Steps

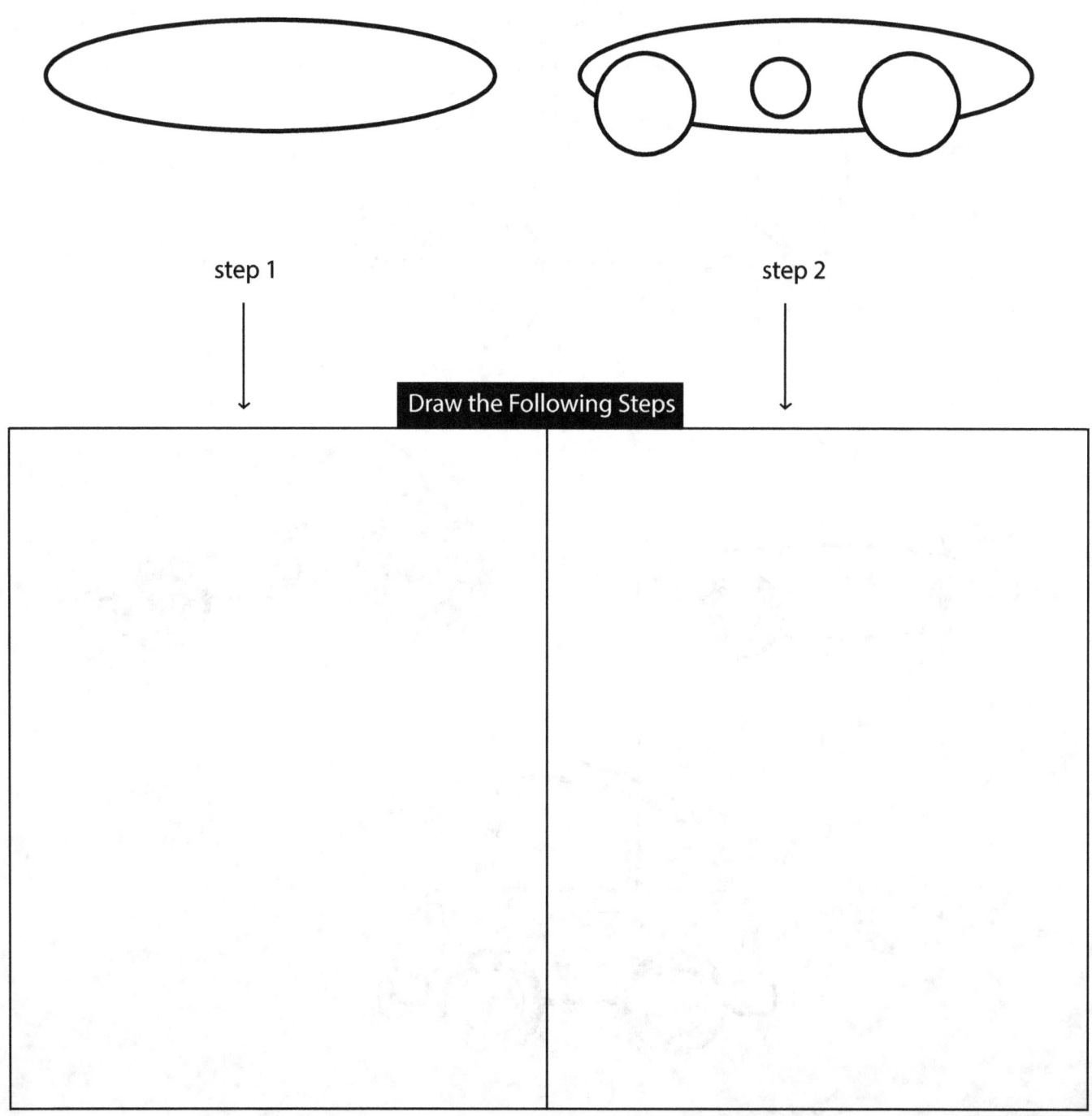

step 1   step 2

Draw the Following Steps

The Steps

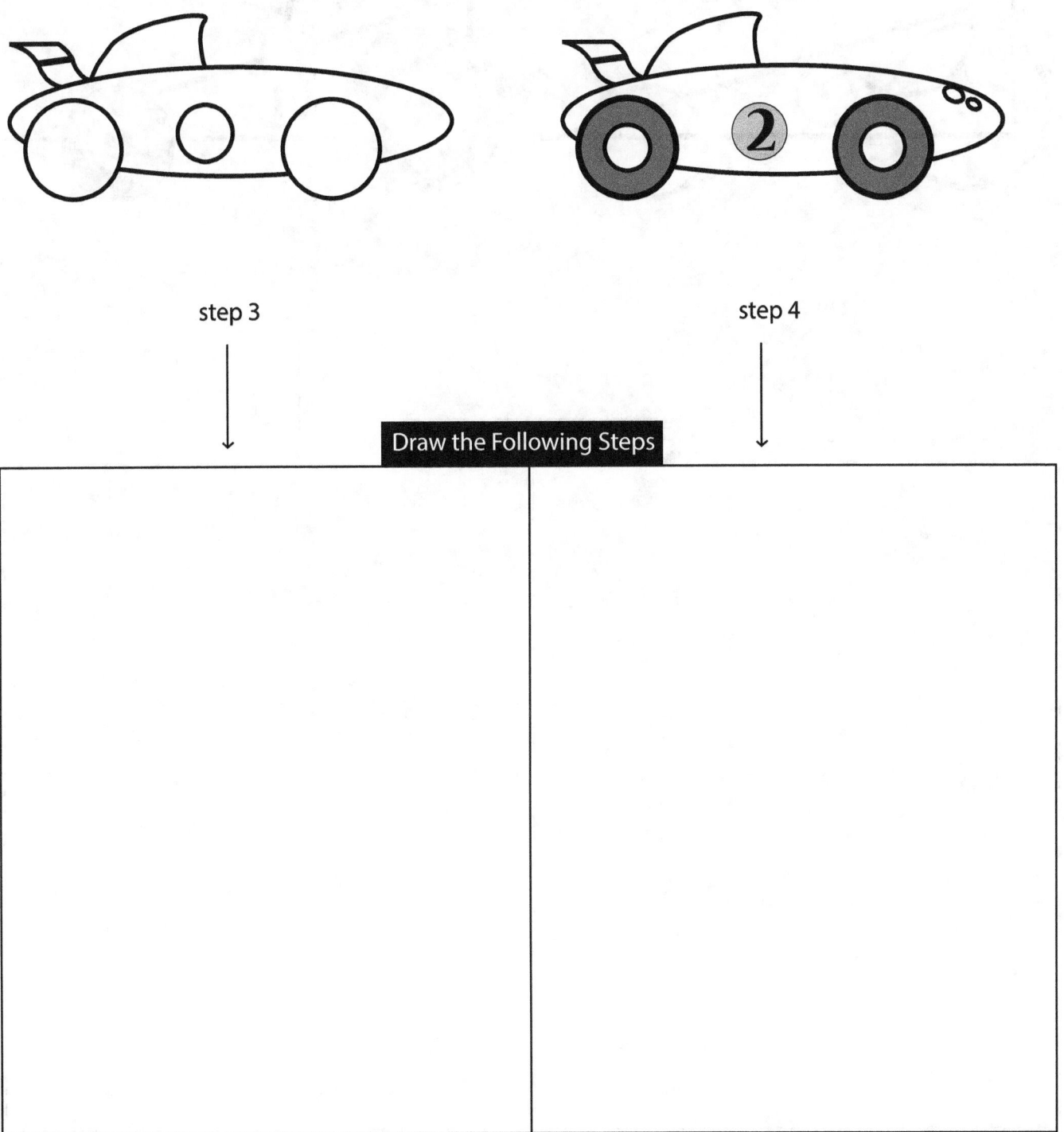

step 3

step 4

Draw the Following Steps

The Steps

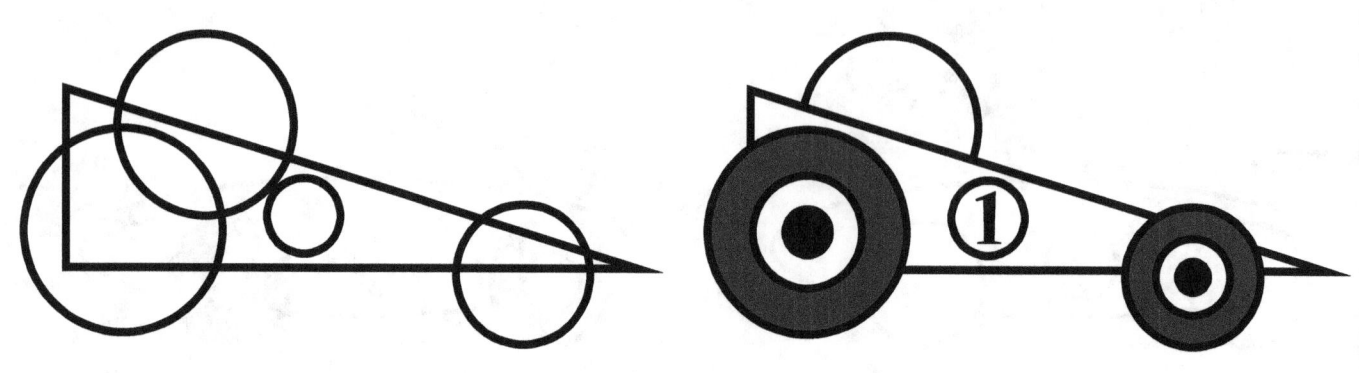

step 1

step 2

Draw the Following Steps

The Steps

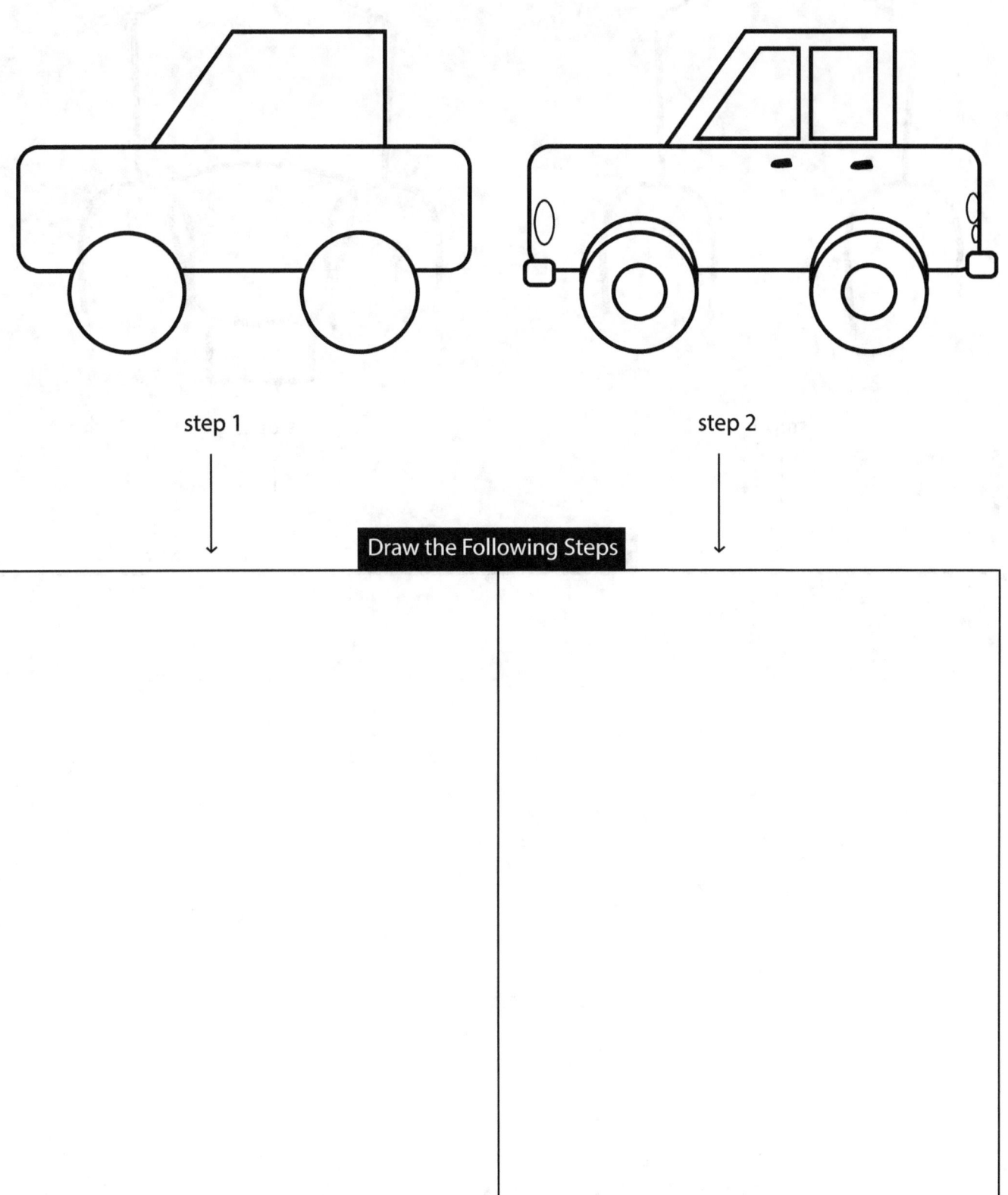

step 1

step 2

Draw the Following Steps

The Steps

step 1

step 2

Draw the Following Steps

The Steps

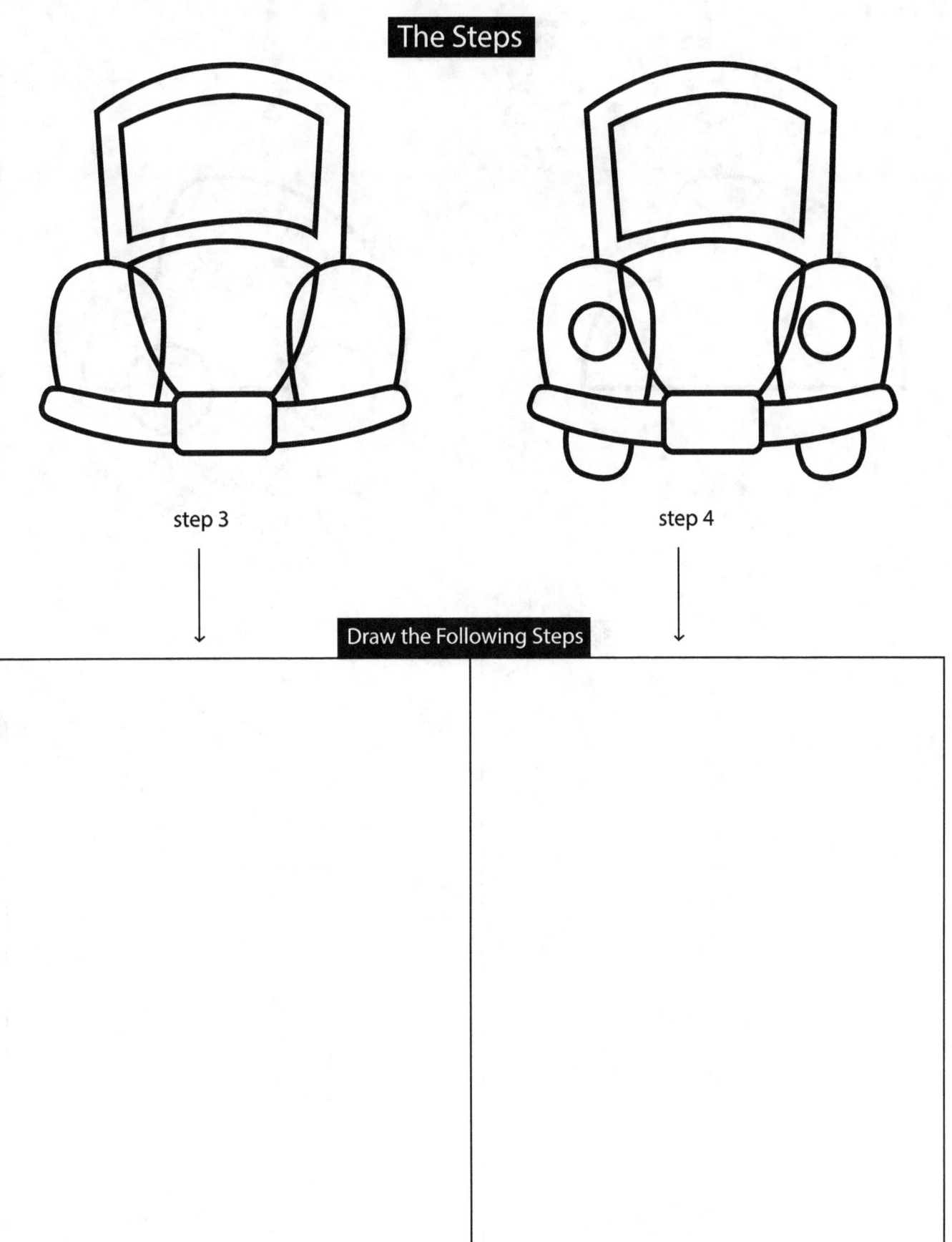

step 3

step 4

Draw the Following Steps

The Steps

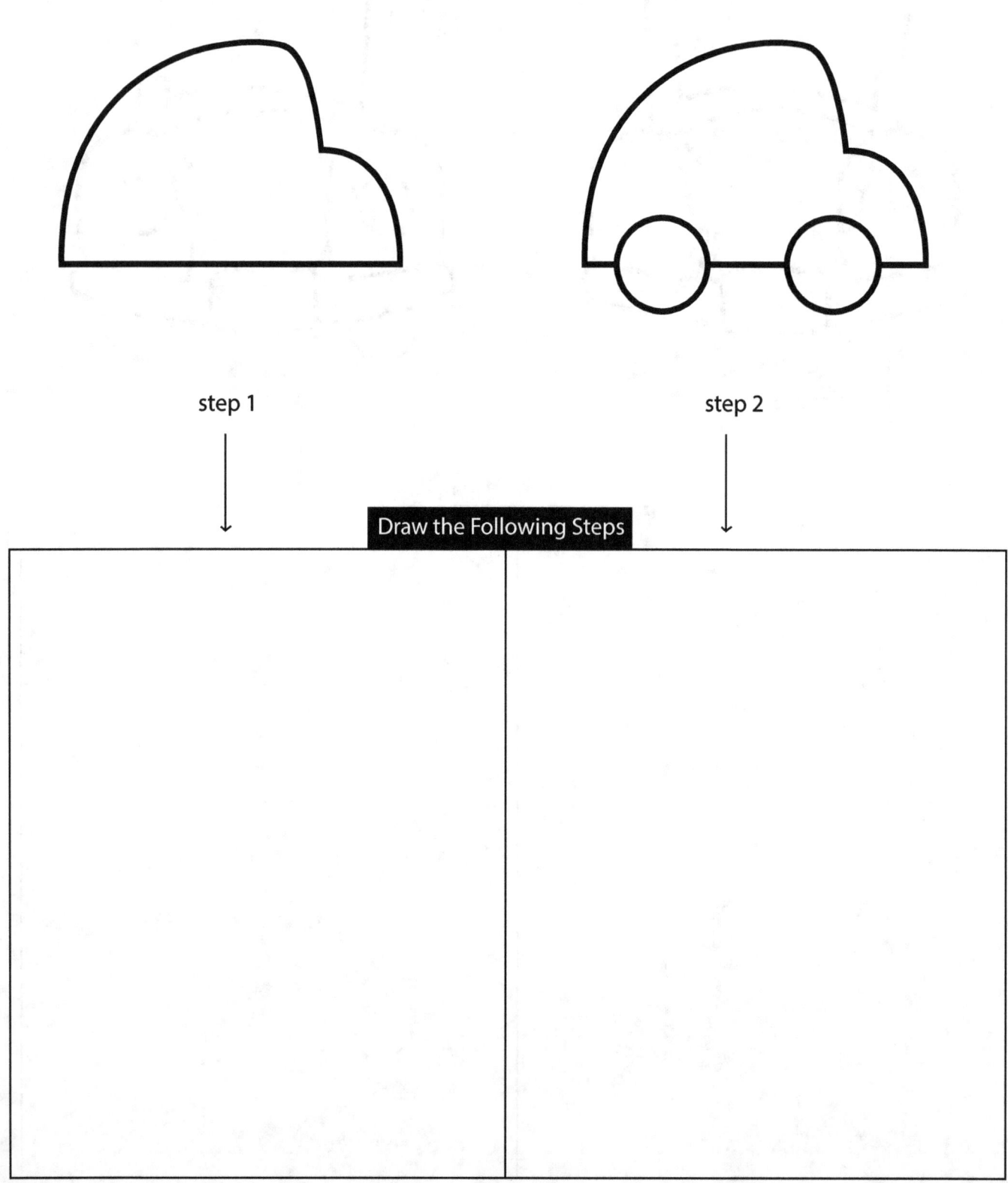

step 1

step 2

Draw the Following Steps

The Steps

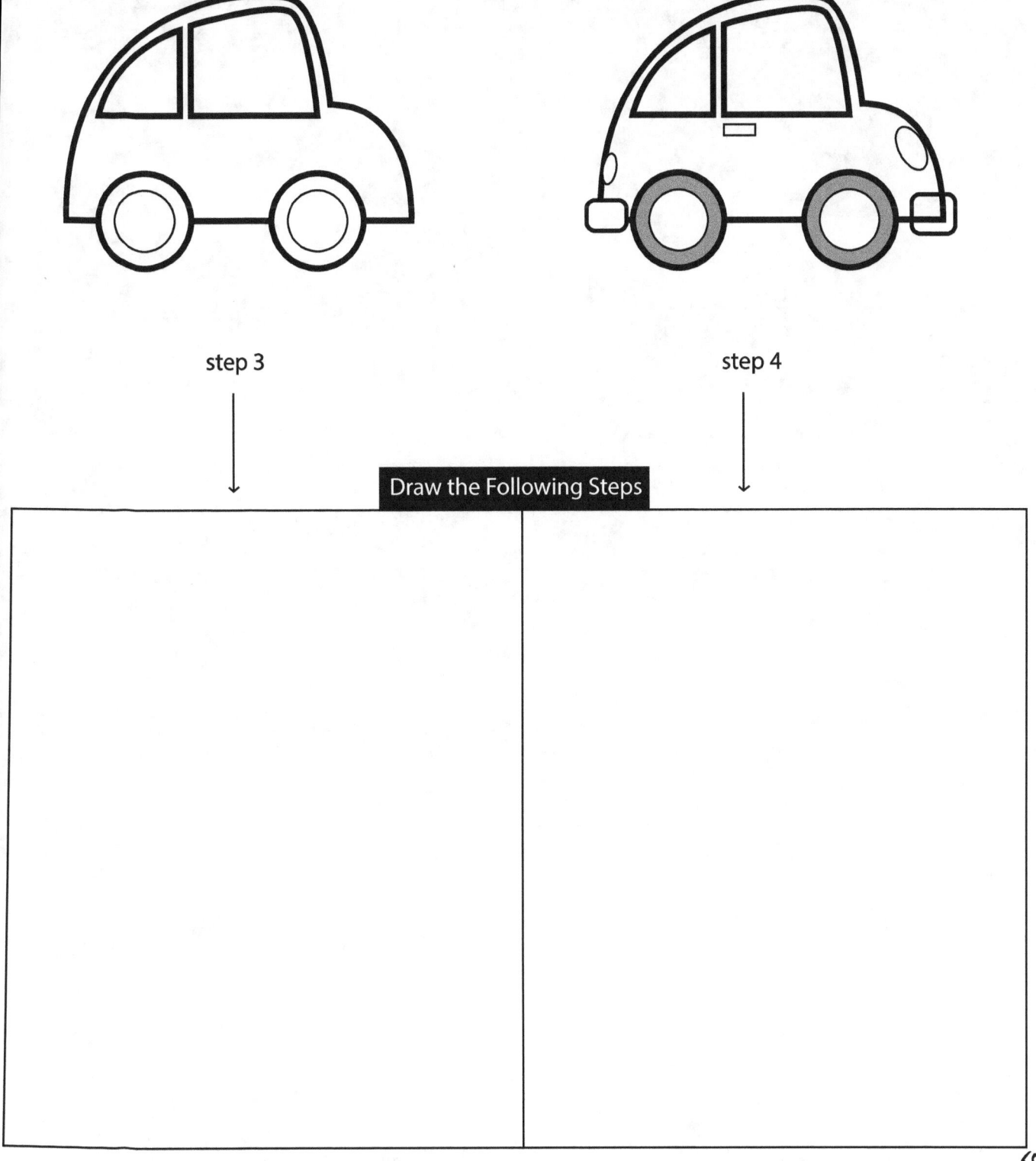

step 3

step 4

Draw the Following Steps

www.ingramcontent.com/pod-product-compliance
Lightning Source LLC
Chambersburg PA
CBHW081537220526
45467CB00010B/3228